The Iranian
Revolution

MILESTONES

IN MODERN WORLD HISTORY

1600 · · · 1750 · · · ·

· · 1940 · · · 2000

The Bolshevik Revolution

The Chinese Cultural
Revolution

The Collapse of
the Soviet Union

D-Day and the Liberation
of France

The End of Apartheid
in South Africa

The Iranian Revolution

The Treaty of Versailles

The Universal Declaration
of Human Rights

MILESTONES
IN MODERN
WORLD HISTORY

1600 · · · 1750 · ·   · · · 1940 · · · 2000

The Iranian Revolution

HEATHER LEHR WAGNER

CHELSEA HOUSE
PUBLISHERS
An imprint of Infobase Publishing

The Iranian Revolution

Copyright © 2010 by Infobase Publishing

Chelsea House
An imprint of Infobase Publishing
132 West 31st Street
New York, NY 10001

Library of Congress Cataloging-in-Publication Data

Wagner, Heather Lehr.
The Iranian Revolution / by Heather Lehr Wagner.
  p. cm.—(Milestones in modern world history)
Includes bibliographical references and index.
ISBN 978-1-60413-490-2 (hardcover)
1. Iran—History—Revolution, 1979—Juvenile literature. I. Title.
DS318.8.W34 2009
955.05'3—dc22   2009022336

Chelsea House books are available at special discounts when purchased in bulk quantities for businesses, associations, institutions, or sales promotions. Please call our Special Sales Department in New York at (212) 967-8800 or (800) 322-8755.

You can find Chelsea House on the World Wide Web at http://www.chelseahouse.com.

Text design by Erik Lindstrom
Cover design by Alicia Post
Composition by Keith Trego
Cover printed by Bang Printing, Brainerd, MN
Book printed and bound by Bang Printing, Brainerd, MN
Date printed: January 2010
Printed in the United States of America

10 9 8 7 6 5 4 3 2 1

This book is printed on acid-free paper.

All links and Web addresses were checked and verified to be correct at the time of publication. Because of the dynamic nature of the Web, some addresses and links may have changed since publication and may no longer be valid.

CONTENTS

1

The Ayatollah Returns

The Air France plane touched down at the airport in Iran's capital city, Tehran, at 9:30 A.M. local time on February 1, 1979. The plane was half full; there had been concern that it might not be able to land, and so Air France had allowed on only half the normal number of passengers to ensure that the plane might safely return to Paris if necessary. There had been many threats against the flight or, more specifically, against one of the passengers on board. Iran was in the midst of a revolution, and the Air France flight was carrying the man many declared was the father of that revolution, Ayatollah Ruhollah Khomeini.

Some 1,500 political and religious leaders had insisted on the right to welcome Khomeini to Tehran, and they thronged the airport terminal, streaming out onto the tarmac when the Air France flight touched down. They were soon joined by

In February 1979, Ayatollah Ruhollah Khomeini, the founder of Iran's Islamic republic, waves to supporters in Tehran shortly after his return from 14 years of exile.

airport workers. As Khomeini appeared at the top of the stairs leading down from the plane, there were screams and cries of *"Allahu Akbar"* (God is great).

To a disinterested observer, it might have been difficult to understand the tremendous emotion generated by the sight of an old, bearded man dressed in the traditional robes and turban of an Islamic leader. But there were no disinterested observers at the airport on that February morning. The hopes of an entire nation rested on the shoulders of a 77-year-old man who had spent the past 14 years in exile actively speaking out against the regime of Iran's ruler, Shah Reza Pahlavi. After months of strikes and protests, the government of the shah had collapsed, and he and his wife had been forced to leave Iran. Now, the *ayatollah* (a title indicating a respected religious leader among Shia Muslims, the dominant branch of Islam in Iran) had returned, and it seemed that most of Iran, having risen up in response to his calls to overthrow the shah's regime, now wanted to personally welcome him home.

Khomeini spoke briefly inside the airport terminal, acknowledging his supporters. "I thank the clergy who have sacrificed so much in this affair," he said. "I thank the students who suffered tragedies. I thank the merchants and traders who suffered. I thank the young of the bazaar, the universities and the theological colleges who offered their blood."[1]

Some 50,000 police tried to hold back the crowds that were pushing their way toward the airport, but they were unable to contain the people clamoring for a glimpse of Khomeini. Seated in an American-made blue-and-white station wagon, Khomeini and his entourage made slow progress along a road lined with crowds desperate to see the ayatollah. The crowd was estimated at nearly 5 million; soon it had surrounded Khomeini's car, some people even jumping up on top of it to see him.

Khomeini was traveling through the streets of Tehran, a city that had changed dramatically in the 14 years he had been away.

(continues on page 12)

"THE PEOPLE HAVE RAISED THEIR VOICES IN PROTEST"

On October 29, 1978, from exile in France, Ayatollah Khomeini spoke to a group of students and Iranians living abroad. Many of his speeches made in exile were recorded and smuggled into Iran. In this excerpt, Khomeini speaks of Iranians' demands for freedom and independence:

From the very beginning of the Islamic movement, . . . up until the present when, praise be to God, it has reached its peak, our aim . . . has been the same, and that is to secure freedom and independence for the Iranian nation. Both these demands are legitimate rights that all human societies, those that is which have not strayed from the path of humanity, recognize. A nation of thirty or thirty-five million people is being suppressed; for fifty years this thirty-million-strong nation has been stifled and repressed and has suffered difficulties in every respect. Throughout this period, its preachers and orators have not been free to speak out on different matters, it has enjoyed neither a free press nor has its radio been a national radio run by the people. . . . But now this thirty-million-strong nation . . . has risen up and is demanding its right. The people are saying that they want to be free and this is a demand that all human societies recognize, for it is a just demand. The Iranian people are not asking for something which is not their right.

Secondly they demand independence. There have been many periods in our history . . . when our country was dominated in all aspects by foreigners. Our economy is now

(continues)

Followers of the Ayatollah Khomeini march in Tehran on
February 6, 1979, a few days after his return from exile in France.

(continued)

disrupted because it is being controlled by foreigners. They are taking our oil and in return they build bases for themselves in Iran. . . . They have kept our education in a state of backwardness; they do not allow our young people to receive a proper education lest some of them begin to oppose what they are doing here. They do not permit our Islamic culture to develop, and through their propaganda, they try to distance the people from Islam . . . they realize that were true Islam put into practice in Iran, or in other countries, the foreigners would have no place there. One of the commands of Islam states that foreigners should not be allowed to interfere in the destiny of Muslims. If the *ulama* of Islam [the Islamic scholars or those who possess religious "learning"] acquire power, they will not permit this command to be forgotten, they will put it into practice. So these two forces, the forces of Islam and the *ulama*, must be defeated (in the view of the foreigners). . . .

However, . . . this uprising . . . in Iran now is becoming more extensive day by day. As we sit here a revolution is unfurling in many Iranian cities, the people have raised their voices in protest, there are clashes and killings. Iran is now gripped by a revolution which like a flood is sweeping away the Shah and destroying the interests of those who have benefited from his rule. Please God it will succeed. We ourselves want to administer this country, which is ours and which has been passed on to us from our ancestors. . . .*

---

* "Speech Number Forty-Nine of the Imam," I.R.I.B. World-service, http://www2.irib.ir/worldservice/imam/speech.

(continued from page 9)

In recent years, the shah had engaged in an ambitious program of construction and modernization intending to transform Iran's capital into the most glamorous and progressive city in the Middle East. Many of those projects had not been completed when the shah's government began to fail, and abandoned cranes and half-built structures gave evidence of a country frozen by revolution, a country seeking someone to tell its people how to resume their lives. For many Iranians, Khomeini was that leader.

Khomeini intended to address his supporters from the Behesht-e Zahra cemetery, Iran's largest, but the crowds soon made it impossible for him to continue the journey 12 miles (19 kilometers) south of Tehran. Eventually a helicopter arrived and transported him the remaining distance.

In the cemetery, Khomeini offered prayers for those who had been killed in the revolution. Standing before some 250,000 fervent supporters, he stated firmly the message that had become the hallmark of his speeches while in exile: The shah did not have the right to rule the Iranian people. The government that had been left in power when the shah fled Iran—led by a prime minister appointed by the shah, Dr. Shahpur Bakhtiar—also had no right to govern. Khomeini then stated, "I will strike with my fists at the mouths of this government. From now on it is I who will name the government."[2]

Within five days after his return, Khomeini held a press conference calling on the people of Iran to support the creation of an Islamic government. Within two weeks, Bakhtiar would be forced to step down, and a man handpicked by Khomeini—Mehdi Bazargan—would become Iran's new prime minister. Within 10 days after Khomeini's return, the army had given up any attempt to defend the old regime. Chaos marked the streets of Tehran, as demonstrators took over the airport, the radio, and the television stations, as well as raided foreign embassies. On April 1, 1979, Khomeini declared that Iran was now an Islamic republic.

In exile, Khomeini had spoken of the need for freedom and democracy in his criticism of the authoritarian rule of the shah. But within two years after his return, Iran had been transformed into a state governed by strict Islamic law, a state of which Khomeini was considered the supreme leader.

THE EMBERS OF REVOLUTION

A complex mix of factors brought about revolution in Iran and led to its evolution from a monarchy to a theocracy (a country governed by rulers who are thought to be divinely guided). One of the principal triggers was a widening gap between the different classes of Iranian society in the 1970s. Steps taken by the shah to capitalize on Iran's position as a chief global exporter of oil had resulted in a dramatic rush of wealth into the country. At the same time, the shah had aggressively pushed a modernization program that increased educational opportunities for many who previously had little or no education, as well as an ambitious program of land reform, dubbed the "White Revolution," that had weakened the wealth and power of many of Iran's upper-class citizens.

The shah's secret police force, known as SAVAK, had terrorized and brutally punished many Iranians, while limiting freedom of speech and other basic human rights. The opulent ceremony and luxuries with which the shah surrounded himself had deepened the resentment of Iran's poorest people. And a series of misjudgments and poorly conceived responses to the crisis only had deepened the gap between the shah's regime and the people it ruled. Khomeini's fiery speeches denouncing the shah and his Western allies, delivered in exile and smuggled into the country on cassette tapes, had found a receptive audience among many groups in Iran that were deeply unhappy with the monarchy, including religious leaders, students, the poor, and even some members of Iran's middle class.

For months, protests ravaged the streets of Tehran and other cities throughout Iran. The response from the shah's police was swift and brutal, sparking more unrest and violence. Strikes in protest of the shah's actions paralyzed the country, making it nearly impossible for people to work, to shop, to travel, or to go about their daily activities.

On January 16, 1979, the shah and his wife, Empress Farah, left Iran, departing from an airport where empty airplanes lined the runways, a result of the work strikes that had crippled the country. The shah spoke briefly to the few members of the Iranian press who had been informed of his departure. He told them that he was feeling tired, that he needed a rest, and that he was taking a trip. He said he did not know when he would return.

When word of his departure reached the people, broadcast on Tehran Radio, the capital was filled with celebrations. Iranians shouted and cheered; car horns blared. Statues of the shah were torn down. For many Iranians, the departure of the shah indicated that the revolution had been a success. The monarchy that had brutalized so many people had been brought down; a new, more representative form of government would take its place.

But the celebration was mixed with uncertainty. The shah had ruled Iran for nearly 37 years; his father had ruled for 16 years before that. Many Iranians had known no other ruler besides a member of the Pahlavi family. The only form of government they knew was one led by a strong, authoritative leader.

And so the crowds who filled the streets of Tehran cheering the departure of the shah and the success of their revolution also called out for the return to Iran of the man they believed could bring about the successful end to the revolution. They cried out for Ayatollah Khomeini to come home and lead them.

The Pahlavi Dynasty

On February 21, 1921, an army of some 3,000 men marched to Tehran to take control of the government. They seized all of the government buildings, the police stations, and all government offices. They announced that their plan was to support their ruler, Ahmad Shah, and to oversee the peaceful withdrawal of British troops from their country. But within a few brief years the shah had been forced, not only to flee the country, but to give up his throne. Power had been consolidated in the hands of the army's commander in chief, Reza Khan, who by 1925 had himself crowned the new shah, Reza Shah Pahlavi.

The roots of the 1979 revolution in Iran can be found in these events more than 50 years earlier. The overthrow of the Pahlavi throne in 1979 contained echoes of the revolution that had brought the family to power. An understanding of the family and its reign is important in understanding the factors that led to its disintegration.

The Pahlavi family that would ultimately surround itself with luxury had humble origins. Reza Khan was an illiterate peasant, noteworthy mainly for his height and his bravery in battle, when he first caught the eye of British officials occupying a land then known as Persia. In ancient times, Persia had been a mighty empire that had conquered the Babylonians and the Egyptians. But the empire did not last, and Persia was conquered by a succession of invaders, including the Greeks, Turks, Afghans, and Russians.

By the early twentieth century, the British were eager to increase their influence in Persia. The country offered access into Asia (especially, in the southeastern region, to British-ruled India), as well as opportunities for trade. It was also rich in oil. Gradually, Russia and Great Britain established an understanding with each other: Northern Persia would be controlled by Russia while the southern region around the Persian Gulf would be subject to British influence.

At this time, a weak shah ruled Persia, but the shah was motivated more by the payments given to him by foreign powers than by a concern for the welfare of his people. When World War I began in 1914, Persia became the site of battles between the Turks, who were allied with the Germans, and British and Russian forces. By the time the war ended in 1918, Great Britain was determined to cement its influence in the Middle East by installing governments that would be friendly to its interests. One of its targets was Persia.

The British approached Persia's ruler, a weak young man named Ahmad Shah, a member of the Qajar family, who was already receiving regular payments from Great Britain in exchange for preserving a "friendly" attitude toward British interests. In exchange for more money and the promise of additional security to protect his hold on power, the shah agreed to sign the Anglo-Persian Treaty on August 9, 1919. The treaty essentially gave Great Britain the right to oversee Persia's development in all areas. British officials would supervise the construction of railroads, the training of the military, Persia's finances, and its taxes. British officials insisted that the arrangement had nothing to do with access to Iran's oil; instead, they claimed to be preparing Persia to transition to independence and to be protecting its people from Russia.

Within Persia, people were unhappy with the amount of foreign influence over the shah and the country, a theme that would be echoed in the revolution of 1979. Attempts were made to overthrow the shah and negotiate a new deal with Russia. Chaos reigned in much of Persia, while Russian and British troops were skirmishing with each other along the borders.

British officials realized that the shah had become too weak to retain power and preserve the powerful alliance they wanted. They began to look around for a different leader—one who was not tied too closely or obviously to British interests, but could seize control and unite the country; perhaps someone with the support of an army.

MILITARY MAN

British officials in Persia knew of only one military division powerful enough—and independent enough—to accomplish their goals. It was the Persian Cossack Brigade, created in 1879 to serve as bodyguards for the shah. The Persian Cossacks contained some 6,000 men, who were patrolling the northern region of the country.

There was one problem with using the Persian Cossacks: it was led by a Russian officer, whose interests could conflict with the British. The British were able to engineer his dismissal, as well as that of his second-in-command. Then they selected the toughest Persian officer they could find, a colonel named Reza Khan, to lead the brigade. One British official described him as "the most manly Persian" he had ever met.[1]

Reza Khan was exceptionally tall (6 feet, 3 inches) and rugged, an illiterate peasant who had nevertheless risen to prominence within the Cossacks for his bravery in battle and for his outspoken criticism of the chaos that had overtaken Persia. Born on March 16, 1878, into a poor family living in a small village in the Elburz Mountains in northern Iran, Khan was in his forties when he assumed command. Reassured by British officials that they would not oppose a peaceful *coup d'etat* (attempt to overthrow the government) if he guaranteed that his army would not take action against either the shah or the British military, Reza Khan readily agreed to the British plan.

On February 21, 1921, Reza Khan led troops into Tehran, seized power, and named himself commander in chief of the armed forces. He then began to rapidly consolidate power in his own hands. He was named minister of war and took command of the police force. Within a short time, the power to maintain order within Persia was not in the hands of the shah or occupying British forces, but in the hands of Reza Khan.

Reza Khan was determined to eliminate any threats to his power and to centralize control in his hands. One threat was the tribal leaders who controlled vast stretches of the countryside, which was principally used for grazing land for animals. Those leaders had made deals with foreign powers that had helped establish British and Russian areas of influence in Persia and weakened the shah's authority. Reza Khan determined to send a clear message that this kind of independent negotiating with foreign powers would no longer be tolerated: He sent an army of 15,000 to Khuzestan in southwestern Iran, at the head of the Persian Gulf, bordering Iraq. Khuzestan had proved fiercely independent in the past, and its leader, or *sheikh*, had been quite willing to negotiate with foreign powers for rights to the land he controlled. Many of the people there spoke Arabic, rather than the Farsi spoken in most of Persia, and the region was rich in oil. Reza Khan's troops came with an invitation for Khuzestan's sheikh to accompany them back to Tehran, an invitation they intended to enforce. Eventually the sheikh agreed to go with them to the capital, where he was held under armed

The shah of Iran, Reza Khan Pahlavi, is shown in a portrait from December 1938. He would rule Iran from 1925 to 1941. His son, Mohammad Reza Pahlavi, would step down as shah in 1979 during the Iranian Revolution.

guard for several years. Without a war, without an execution, Reza Khan had sent a clear message to all tribal leaders that he was in charge.

Reza Khan was inspired by the efforts of Kemal Atatürk, the charismatic leader of Turkey, who had recently led a revolution to transform his country into a modern, Westernized, and secular (nonreligious) republic. Reza Khan had similar hopes for Persia, and he mimicked some of the steps Atatürk had taken, such as overseeing plans for industrialization, requiring Persians to take family names (last names), and eliminating many of the honorary titles that had sharply divided society into classes in the past.

For his own family name, Reza Khan chose *Pahlavi*. The name emphasized his connection to the country's past; Pahlavi was an ancient language in Persia. It also held more subtle meaning—*pahlavan* is the Persian word for "champion."

Reza Khan Pahlavi next seized the shah's throne. The weak shah had fled Persia several years earlier, and on October 31, 1925, the Parliament officially ended his reign. On December 12 of that same year, Reza Khan officially became the new ruler, earning the title Reza Shah. His coronation took place on April 25, 1926. As part of the ceremony, his oldest son, seven-year-old Mohammad Reza Pahlavi, was named crown prince.

SON AND HEIR

Mohammad was one of 11 children born to Reza Khan. He and his twin sister, Ashraf, were born on October 26, 1919, nearly two years before his father led his victorious march on Tehran. Their mother was Reza Shah's second wife, Taj-ol Molouk. Ashraf was outgoing and outspoken; her twin brother was far quieter. A few weeks after his father's coronation, Mohammad caught typhoid fever and nearly died. As an adult, he spoke of his recovery as miraculous, the result of a dream in which Ali, the son-in-law of the prophet Muhammad, handed him a bowl of cool liquid to drink. The next morning his fever was gone.

He would later speak of other brushes with death as evidence that he was blessed.

He was weak and ill for much of his childhood. His father was a strong personality, not only when ruling Iran but also at home. Mohammad would later write of his father's "piercing eyes that arrested anybody who met him. Those eyes could make a strong man shrivel up inside."[2] It took many years before the young Mohammad felt comfortable speaking frankly in front of his father.

Because of his lack of education, Reza Shah was determined that his children would receive the best education possible. Mohammad, at the age of six, learned to speak French from a French governess and then attended Tehran's military school before being sent away, at the age of 12, to attend the elite Le Rosey School in Lausanne, Switzerland. He did not return to Iran for five years. He quickly developed an attraction for Western history, philosophy, and customs. This influence would affect him for the rest of his life.

When he was 17, Mohammad Pahlavi finally returned home. His father's modernization campaign had dramatically changed the country during his absence. "It was like visiting a different country," he later recalled. "I recognized nothing. . . . My father had razed Tehran's old walls. Streets were paved and asphalted. The city had begun to take on the look and style of a European capital."[3] Even the name of the country had changed while Mohammad was in Switzerland. In 1935, Reza Shah officially proclaimed that the name of his kingdom was no longer Persia. Instead, it was to be called Iran, a name that harkened back to the land's distant past, reflecting the name of an ancient nomadic tribe that had moved into the land from Central Asia around 1500 B.C.

Reza Shah's modernization campaign had influenced all areas of Iranian life. He had overseen the reform of the country's corrupt legal system, following the example of that used in Europe. This alienated many of Iran's religious leaders, who wanted Iran to be governed based on traditional Islamic principles through the legal system known as *sharia*, which is binding on all Muslims. Reza Shah further alienated Islamic traditionalists when he passed an edict in 1935 that banned women from wearing the *chador*, the heavy, floor-length black garment that covered much of the female body and was considered by many Muslims an important part of dressing modestly. After the edict banning the chador was passed, women wearing the garment were no longer allowed into taxis, buses, or movie theaters, and police would forcibly remove it from women wearing it in public.

Reza Shah also focused on education for his people, just as he had done for his own children. New teachers were trained, and schools were opened to both girls and boys and legally required for all children aged 6 to 13. New secondary schools were built, military and teachers colleges were constructed, and the University of Tehran opened in 1935.

Mohammad now began the nearly impossible task of preparing to become his father's successor. Still intimidated by Reza Shah, Mohammad attended Tehran's Officers' Academy and learned to fly. His father's influence also extended to his choice of a bride. When Mohammad was 19, his father decided it was time for him to marry and began a search for an appropriate wife, with a focus on someone who would provide a strategic alliance for Iran's crown prince.

Reza Shah settled on the 17-year-old sister of Egypt's King Farouk as the best bride for his son. The two married in the spring of 1939. A daughter, Princess Shahnaz, was born the following year.

ABDICATION

When World War II broke out in September 1939, Reza Shah declared that Iran would remain neutral. That soon became impossible. British and Russian forces launched a combined attack on Iran early on the morning of August 25, 1941. Soon, more than 100,000 British Empire forces (mainly from India) entered Iran from the north, south, and west, seizing ports and oil fields. Within three days, Iran surrendered. Reza Shah decided to abdicate, telling his son Mohammad, "I cannot be the nominal head of an occupied land, to be dictated to by a minor English or Russian officer."[4] He was forced into exile, finally ending up in South Africa, where he died on July 26, 1944.

British troops occupying Iran were not sure whether to allow the 22-year-old Mohammad to succeed his father. They tried to locate a member of the Qajar dynasty—the family that had ruled Iran before being forced out by Reza Shah—but discovered that the only likely successor was living abroad and did not speak any Farsi, Iran's language. They agreed to install Mohammad Reza Pahlavi as the new shah, but his powers would be severely limited. Great Britain occupied most of the south; Russia was in control in the north.

The young shah faced a nearly impossible task: following the reign of his dominant and powerful father, attempting to rule an occupied country, and dealing with a country suffering the effects of war. He determined to make alliances with some of the people his father had opposed, including religious leaders. He loosened restrictions on clothing, so that women once again were seen in the streets wearing the chador. He agreed to mark Ramadan, the holy month of fasting observed by devout Muslims, by enforcing restrictions on the consumption of food and drink. And he overturned the restrictions his father had imposed on pilgrimages to the holy city of Mecca in Saudi Arabia—a journey all able-bodied Muslims must make at least once.

The shah also decided to form an alliance with a foreign nation powerful enough to challenge Iran's British and Russian occupiers: the United States. The Americans soon encouraged Great Britain and Russia to sign a treaty agreeing to withdraw from Iran after the war, which ended in 1945. During this stressful time the shah and his wife, Princess Fawzia, were divorced. In 1949, he married Soraya Esfandiari, the 18-year-old daughter of an Iranian father and German mother.

OIL POLITICS

Oil was first discovered in Iran in 1908 and had been a factor in Iran's relationships with foreign powers ever since. The Anglo-Iranian Oil Company (AIOC) was formed shortly thereafter, and the British representatives wooed the Qajar shah until he provided them with a 51 percent ownership in the company. Reza Shah had tried to break this British control over Iranian oil, and conflict had long existed over whether Iran was receiving a fair share of the profits from its oil. AIOC refused to allow any Iranians to go through its records to determine how much money was being made from Iran's resource. Senior jobs in the company were reserved for British technicians.

By 1951, this conflict would erupt in a challenge to Mohammad Reza Pahlavi's rule in the form of a 69-year-old Iranian member of Parliament, Mohammed Mosaddeq. Mosaddeq had long opposed the rule of the Pahlavis, dating back to the elevation of Reza Shah as ruler. His family had been wealthy landowners who served as ministers to the Qajar family. He had been educated in Switzerland and served in government before Reza Shah seized power. He had little regard for the Pahlavis, but even less for the British.

In Parliament, Mosaddeq began to issue calls for nationalization of the AIOC. Other politicians soon joined him, as well as another important ally—Ayatollah Kashani, an Islamic religious leader who opposed the liberal policies of the Pahlavis and Great Britain's presence in Iran. Bolstered by the support of religious and political leaders, Mosaddeq was able to lead a movement in Parliament that called for the nationalization of the AIOC on March 15, 1951. On April 29, his popularity continuing to rise, Mosaddeq was elected prime minister.

Located in the Middle East between the nations of Iraq, Afghanistan, and Pakistan and bordering the Persian Gulf, Iran is rich in natural resources, most notably petroleum and natural gas.

Many Westerners viewed Mosaddeq as eccentric and even unstable. But Iranians admired his ability to stand up to the British at a time when the shah was viewed as weak and too closely allied with the West. This new leader ordered all British AIOC employees out of the country, a move that would prove problematic when it became clear that the Iranian employees lacked the skills and training to operate the refinery and wells or to manage the company. At the same time, furious at Mosaddeq's actions, Great Britain began a boycott of Iranian oil, causing oil revenue to drop and creating a financial crisis in Iran. Soon, government employees, teachers, and policemen were receiving IOUs rather than paychecks.

As the Iranian economy began to collapse, Mosaddeq ordered the shah's mother and sister—viewed by many as the powers behind the throne—to leave Iran. He dismissed the Senate and the Supreme Court and imposed martial law. The shah seemed helpless and powerless. In August 1953, he tried to arrest Mosaddeq, but instead the prime minister arrested the messenger who had been sent to arrest him. Next, a group of army officers was sent to seize Mosaddeq. They failed.

When the shah learned of these failures early in the morning of August 16, he knew his own life was in danger. He woke his wife and prepared to leave the country. He flew the small plane himself, first to Baghdad, the capital of Iraq, and then on to Rome, where the Iranian embassy refused to grant shelter to the shah and his wife. They had little money and had had time only to grab a few clothes. They checked into a Rome hotel, surrounded by paparazzi intent on photographing them during this desperate time.

The shah held several press conferences, each time stating firmly that he believed that he was Iran's legal and constitutional ruler and that he had left the country only to avoid bloodshed. Luckily for the shah, his American allies believed him to be a more reliable friend to the United States than the unpredictable Mosaddeq. They also believed that, if they could restore him to power, he could help tilt Iran's policies—and its oil—toward U.S. interests.

For this reason, the U.S. Central Intelligence Agency (CIA) decided to pay large groups of Iranians to take to the streets in public displays of support for the shah. Soon, Iranian soldiers joined the protestors, increasing the size and scope of the pro-shah support in the streets of Tehran. On August 19, 1953, word reached the shah in Rome that Mosaddeq had been

FOREIGN DEPENDENCE
ON IRANIAN OIL

Oil has played a critical role in Iran's internal politics and foreign policy since 1908, when the British adventurer William Knox D'Arcy first discovered it there. The discovery led to the formation of the Anglo-Iranian Oil Company (AIOC), following negotiations with the shah, who gave his British allies a 51 percent ownership in the company in a contract scheduled to last 60 years. Great Britain oversaw construction of a major oil refinery in southwestern Iran that would become one of the largest in the world.

Unrest about the perceived unfair profits Great Britain was receiving from Iranian oil led to nationalization of the AIOC in 1951 and the subsequent boycotting of Iranian oil by the British government and its citizens. When the new shah, Mohammad Reza Pahlavi, fled the country and the economy teetered on the brink of collapse, the United States offered assistance and support for the shah. America provided

overthrown and that the shah's army once again controlled the capital. Princess Soraya burst into tears; her husband stated, "I knew that they loved me."[5]

The shah quickly returned to Iran. He had learned many critical lessons during his brief time in exile. He resolved never to allow any elements within Iran to grow powerful enough to challenge his rule. He also was determined to cement his alliance with the United States, convinced that his security depended heavily on American support. In his memoir, *Answer to History*, the shah, reflecting on Mosaddeq's downfall, noted:

programs to train Iranian oil workers and became a new market for the oil that would be produced. This oil revenue provided the shah and his family with vast wealth and the resources to fund his efforts to modernize Iran, some of the very factors that would contribute to a growing divide among Iran's classes and the social unrest that led to revolution.

Western dependence on Iranian oil continues to this day. The United States, following decades of conflict with Iran after the revolution, no longer imports oil from Iran. Neither does Great Britain. Germany imports about 1 percent of its oil from Iran; France, about 6 percent; and Italy, 9 percent. Japan and China are far more dependent, receiving about 12 percent of their oil from Iran. Other countries importing Iranian oil are India, South Korea, Turkey, South Africa, Taiwan, and Greece.*

Iran is the second-largest oil producer in OPEC (Organization of the Petroleum Exporting Countries) and the fourth-largest crude-oil exporter in the world.

---

*Dafna Linzer, "U.S. Urges Financial Sanctions on Iran," *Washington Post*, May 29, 2006, p. A1.

In any country a head of government to be effective must do something positive. [He] . . . betrayed the common people of Iran by promising them a better deal and then sabotaging his own promises. The people lived for a time on these promises. Then they realized that no matter how dramatically promises are put, you cannot feed your children upon them. They also saw that their native country was disintegrating before their eyes. So the people, especially the common people, rebelled.[6]

3

Sign of God

Located in the center of Iran, along the trade route from the Persian Gulf ports in the south to Iran's capital, Tehran, in the north, the village of Khomein was a small but prosperous place at the beginning of the twentieth century. Water from the melting snow of the Zagros Mountains provided all that the village needed, and the land around Khomein was marked by orchards, land for grazing, and farmland dotted with fields of grain. The goods moving along the trade route kept the village market supplied.

On the eastern edge of the village stood a house with a large garden. It was here that Ruhollah Khomeini was born on September 24, 1902. Members of his family believed they were directly descended from the prophet Muhammad; Ruhollah's father, Mostafa, was a senior cleric in Iran's Shiite hierarchy.

Ruhollah, the third-eldest son, was one of the family's six children. Because of Mostafa's position as a senior cleric, the family enjoyed a certain amount of influence in the community.

The region in which they lived was one of the more lawless provinces that Reza Khan would bring under control in the 1920s. Because there was no strong central government at the time of Ruhollah's birth, many in the community turned to Mostafa for protection and aid when disputes arose over land or water, or when the shah sent emissaries to collect taxes.

Mostafa's prominence and willingness to offer armed protection to those in need no doubt contributed to his death in March 1903, less than six months after Ruhollah's birth. At the age of 47 Mostafa was shot and killed while traveling on the road from Khomein to Arak. There are differing accounts as to why he was murdered, but most suggest he was traveling to Arak to seek the help of the provincial governor based there in resolving a conflict and that one of the parties to the dispute murdered him before he could reach the governor.

Young Ruhollah grew up in a busy, noisy household. He lived with his mother, aunt, brothers, and sisters in a large two-story home that overlooked the river on one side and gardens on the other. A portion of the family's estate was rented out to the provincial governor's deputy, who used the first floor as offices and whose guards were housed on the second floor.

Ruhollah was high-spirited and energetic, taller than most boys his age, and strong. He enjoyed sports and games, especially wrestling and leapfrog. When he was seven, he was sent to a local school, a *maktab* (place of writing, in Arabic), where he learned the alphabet, the Koran (the book of sacred writings believed by Muslims to be revelations made to the prophet Muhammad by God, or Allah), and religious stories. Students learned by memorization and repetition; the teacher (usually a woman or elderly cleric) would speak a line and the children would all repeat it. After spending a brief time in the maktab,

Ruhollah was sent to a school in Khomein where he studied math, history, geography, basic science, and Persian language and literature. Private tutors were hired to train him in calligraphy, Arabic grammar, and theology.

A cholera epidemic struck Iran in 1918, and both Ruhollah's mother and aunt died from it, just as the 16-year-old Ruhollah was preparing to enter seminary to continue his religious training. Initially he planned to study in Isfahan, a center of Shiite learning for several centuries located not far from Khomein. However, when Ruhollah learned that a superior theological

WHAT DOES IT MEAN TO BE A SHIITE?

In Iran, most Muslims are Shiites. Their faith has several important differences from that of the Sunni Muslims, who make up much of the rest of the Muslim world. The dispute between mainstream Sunni Muslims and the Shiite branch centers on the question of who was the proper successor to Islam's most important prophet, Muhammad. The very names of these two facets of Islam reflect this dispute: *Shiite* comes from the term *Shi'at Ali* (meaning the faction of Ali, Muhammad's cousin), while *Sunni* means "obeying tradition" in Arabic.

The dispute over who would become Muhammad's political and spiritual successor began in A.D. 632, the year the prophet died. Sunni Muslims felt that Muhammad's successor should be chosen following the system that had been in place before the prophet: The community's elders should meet and select the next leader. But a small minority of Muslims disagreed, college was being set up in nearby Sultanabad-Arak, he decided to enroll there instead.

SEMINARY STUDENT

Ruhollah studied under Sheikh Abdolkarim Ha'eri, who had located his school away from larger cities because he believed that clerics should not be involved in politics. At the time, in Iranian cities known for their connection to Shiism like Najaf, or in Tehran, politics were dominating daily life, and there were frequent protests against British influence in the country.

believing that instead the wishes of Muhammad himself should be followed. The prophet had stated that his first cousin and son-in-law, Ali, should be his successor. These were the Shi'at Ali, or Shiites.

For some 30 years the debate continued over whether Ali was the legitimate successor, until Ali was assassinated. Ali's son, Hosein, launched a rebellion against the Sunni leaders until, some 20 years later, he too was assassinated. This is the beginning of a history of conflict between Shiites and Sunnis that would last for 13 centuries and still plays out in the Middle East.

There are other elements of Islam unique to Shiites. They believe in the importance of imams, spiritual leaders who receive divine guidance to interpret the teachings of the Koran. They believe there have been 12 imams since Ali. Their interpretation of Islam also centers on the importance of discussion and debate, based on the idea that informed arguments can lead to a better understanding of Muhammad's writings and prophecies. This policy of debate and discussion was a critical aspect of the religious training of Ruhollah Khomeini.

Ha'eri's attitude—that religious leaders should remain above political debate—was different from that of many of his peers, and Ruhollah himself, in his later years, would adopt a position precisely opposite that of his teacher.

But Ruhollah would remain heavily influenced by Ha'eri in other ways. Ha'eri shunned material possessions and lived a simple life focused on religious practices and predictable routine. He took daily walks alone, unlike many clerics of the time who emphasized their importance and status by surrounding themselves with supporters and even armed guards.

As a member of his class and family, it was expected that Ruhollah would study at a seminary, or *madreseh* as it is known in the Islamic world. This did not necessarily mean that he was committing to a life spent in religious pursuits. But while he studied under Ha'eri, Ruhollah began to find his calling in religious learning and decided to dedicate his life to religious study. This involved a public commitment in which he exchanged the skullcap and short jacket he would ordinarily have worn for the turban, the *qaba* (a long coat worn indoors and outdoors), and the *aba* (a floor-length cloak, usually black, worn over the *qaba* outdoors). Because members of his family were believed to be descended from the prophet Muhammad, Ruhollah's turban was black (those who cannot trace their family origins to Muhammad wear white turbans). After his public commitment to religious study, Ruhollah was known as Seyyed (an honorary title given to descendants of Muhammad) Ruhollah Musavi Khomeini.

In 1921, Ha'eri decided to move his religious school to Qom, a large city 90 miles (144 kilometers) south of Tehran that has traditionally been a place of Shiite learning and houses an important Shia shrine. Great excitement surrounded the plans to build a major religious institution with teachers in all branches of Islamic learning. Soon, Ha'eri was joined not only by the clerics who had taught with him before, but also leading clerics from other cities.[1]

But Ha'eri's plans for a great center of religious learning were at odds with those of Reza Khan, who had ridden into Tehran several months earlier and seized power. Within several years he would introduce laws intended to transform Iran into a secular state and remove much of the power held by the clergy, while challenging many of the social laws and customs that were central to Islam. The culmination would come when Reza Shah's wife traveled to the shrine at Qom and appeared there unveiled. The ayatollah in Qom delivered a sermon criticizing the shah and encouraging protests. The shah, accompanied by armed forces, traveled immediately to Qom and had the ayatollah arrested. Ha'eri, in an effort to calm down the situation, issued a religious edict (a *fatwa*) forbidding any discussion of the events.[2]

As a student at the new school, Ruhollah Khomeini began his day in the predawn hours, with morning prayers and the first class of the day (a lecture lasting one or two hours). After this there would be a light breakfast and more classes. Students decided which lectures they would attend. They were also expected to spend time memorizing the Koran and reading history, poetry (both Persian and Arabic), and philosophy.

Khomeini began preparations to become a jurist or interpreter of religious law. He studied *sharia*, the Islamic law—its substance, sources, and the basic principles on which legal decisions were made. Over several years, he progressed from memorization and lectures to more interactive studies in which he worked privately with a skilled tutor, graduating to studies with Ha'eri himself. These studies involved lively debate as part of the process of forming enough knowledge and confidence of the Koran and the law to decide the proper legal ruling for any situation.

It was a rigorous and challenging process, which only a few students are able to achieve. At the end, the student's teacher (or teachers) must issue an official permission stating that the student is qualified to interpret the law, either in a specific area or—for the exceptional student like Khomeini—in all areas of Islamic law. Khomeini received this official permission around 1936, when he was about 33 or 34 and about 16 years after he had begun his religious training. Because of this rigorous training and his mastery of it, he was automatically admitted to the higher ranks of clergy and given the title of *ayatollah* (meaning "sign of God").

RELIGIOUS TEACHER

As he was completing his studies, Khomeini was teaching classes in Qom. He also had married. When he was 27, in 1929, he decided to marry Khadijeh Saqafi, the 15-year-old daughter of a wealthy Tehran cleric. She initially said "no," but after a dream in which the prophet Muhammad's daughter appeared to her and told her to marry Khomeini, she changed her mind.[3] She would become his only wife, and the marriage would last 60 years.

In Qom, Khomeini also began to publicly speak out against Reza Shah. He and many of the other clerics were outraged at the shah's modernization program that was compelling Iranians to adopt Western styles of clothing and, particularly disturbing, forcing women to stop wearing the veil. The police enforced the dress code by fining offenders or even snatching the veil from women who dared to wear it.

Iranian activist Sattareh Farman Farmaian, who had been a young girl in a traditional, aristocratic Iranian family during the time of these reforms, wrote of the impact of these new laws on her parents. The veil was considered important to modesty; for her father "to allow strange men to gape at his wives in public was shameful in the extreme. . . . To my mother, it was exactly as if he had insisted that she parade naked in the street."[4] Ultimately, her mother (like many traditional Iranian women) spent more and more time at home.

Khomeini became a popular speaker, often choosing public venues to denounce the prevailing moral failing of most

A 1927 portrait of Ruhollah Khomeini at the age of 25, before he became ayatollah.

Iranians. He delivered his speeches on Thursday or Friday (the days similar to the "weekend" in the West) to ensure that many people would hear him speak. But senior clerics chose to avoid confrontation with the shah, and Khomeini at the time was not senior enough to choose open defiance or to break with the respected clerical leadership.

In 1941, Allied forces invaded Iran, and Reza Khan was forced to abdicate. The early years of the reign of the new shah, Mohammed Reza Pahlavi, were a time when many clerics tried to regain some of the power they had lost under Reza Shah. Some chose to accomplish this by attempting to cooperate with the new shah. But Khomeini remained fiercely opposed to any efforts to secularize Iran. In the postwar years, Khomeini built a reputation as a respected teacher, and became known as one of the leading religious instructors in Qom. Hundreds of people attended his lectures; his former students could be found throughout Iran and even abroad. They were local clerics, preachers, and teachers in their communities. As the new shah tightened his grip on power, Khomeini seemed a very unlikely threat.

Modernization and Reform

For most of the 1950s, Shah Mohammad Reza Pahlavi focused on cementing his power and authority. With assistance from the United States, he began to build a modern intelligence force in Iran. Known as SAVAK (*Sazman-e Ettela'at va Amniat-e Keshvar*, a Farsi name meaning Organization of National Security and Information), this secret police force, whose aim was to eliminate any external or internal threat to his reign, would eventually become symbolic of all that was wrong with the monarchy in Iran because its members tortured and even executed anyone opposed to the shah.

To ensure that the Pahlavi dynasty would continue after he was gone, the shah also became increasingly concerned about his need for a male heir. He had a daughter from his first marriage to Queen Fawzia, which had ended in divorce. His second

In this April 1951 photo, an Iranian refinery burns away oil impurities. Following World War II, the shah used money earned by the oil industry to increase military spending and modernize Iran.

marriage, to Queen Soraya, also ended in divorce after seven years when she failed to produce a child. In 1959, the 39-year-old shah married 21-year-old Farah Dibas, the daughter of a wealthy Iranian family who was studying architecture in Paris when she met the shah. "I had been brought up to venerate the king from childhood," she later recalled. "To me his mission gave him an aura that placed him high above the ordinary run of mortals."[1] The new queen would soon give birth to a son: Crown Prince Reza was born on October 31, 1960. The couple would later have another son and two daughters.

After Iranian oil fields were rebuilt following World War II, production was divided among several foreign firms while Iran retained control of its oil resources. Iran also sold the rights to explore and pump oil in new areas of Iran, including offshore. All of this meant a steady increase in Iranian oil revenue, from $90 million in 1955 to $285 million in 1960 to $482 million in 1964.[2]

The shah also focused on increasing the size of Iran's military. In the 10 years after his return from Italy, he nearly doubled the number of men serving in the military, from 120,000 to 200,000 men. At the same time, he more than quadrupled the military's annual budget—from $42 million in 1953 to $187 million in 1962.[3] Much of this came from millions of dollars in U.S. aid, given in part to strengthen Iran against hostile actions by the Soviet Union and other anti-Western activity in the Middle East.

LAND REFORM

In the 1960s, land reform became the focus of the shah's effort to modernize Iran. The plan, formally known as "The Revolution of the Shah and the People" and informally known as the "White Revolution," featured programs to address the inequitable distribution of land, introduce profit sharing for workers, privatize state factories, and create a "Literacy Corps" made up of recent college graduates who would go into the countryside to teach reading and writing to those who were illiterate. Later, the program would expand to include plans for a "Health Corps," to improve rural health services and educate more health-care workers and to establish rural courts of justice.

These principles were intended to deal with some of the factors that prevented Iran from evolving into the modern nation the shah envisioned. In 1963, when the White Revolution was introduced, only a few hundred families controlled nearly all of the land in Iran. Some three-quarters of all Iranians lived and worked as peasants, many living in primitive homes in rural communities. They enthusiastically supported the ambitious scope of the White Revolution. The shah's program to modernize Iran also won support from many women, who were granted the right to vote in February 1963. However, since Iran lacked fair elections or powerful political parties, the right to vote had little meaning.

But not coincidentally, the White Revolution also was designed to challenge the power of Iran's wealthy landowners and tribal chiefs who had controlled much of life in Iran and who posed a threat to the shah. That proved to be a miscalculation on the part of the shah. By alienating the wealthy, aristocratic class—who traditionally had supported the shah and his policies—the shah deprived himself of important allies when other forces challenged his regime.

The White Revolution also created a deeper rift between the shah and the religious leaders in Iran. Many of the most important religious leaders came from wealthy families—the very families whose land and assets were threatened by the White Revolution. In addition, many of the Shiite clerics were supported directly by donations from wealthy families. The White Revolution threatened the income of these clerics, as well as their ability to maintain their schools and facilities to train future religious leaders. They objected to granting women the right to vote, and they began to speak out against the shah's program.

Among the loudest objectors was Ayatollah Ruhollah Khomeini. He began to openly criticize the White Revolution in speeches and writings, labeling it "a serious threat to Islam."[4] He attacked the shah for his ties to the United States and Israel. His words sparked some of his most fervent supporters to take to the streets of Qom in protest; the shah responded by traveling to Qom. Khomeini instructed his supporters to close their offices and shops and remain indoors during the shah's visit. At a ceremony, several peasants were presented with deeds of land to demonstrate how the shah's program would benefit the people. Then the shah went to the microphone and angrily denounced Iran's religious establishment as backward and irrelevant: "They were always a stupid and reactionary bunch whose brains have not moved. . . . They think life is about getting something for nothing, eating and sleeping. . . . They don't want to see this country develop."[5]

The debate over the shah's modernization program would force many Iranians to take sides, either in support of the shah or in support of the religious leaders. It also would propel Khomeini to the national stage.

THE AYATOLLAH SPEAKS OUT

It was not simply speeches and writings that ensured Khomeini a national pulpit. In those early years he demonstrated his skill at rallying supporters to take action and to encourage demonstrations and protest. At the same time, the government launched an intensive propaganda campaign against the religious leader. Newspapers criticized the clerics for being out of touch or overly conservative. Posters supporting the shah appeared on the streets.

Khomeini responded by widening his criticism to include the changing roles of women in Iranian society. He criticized the appointment of women as judges. The conflict culminated with a speech Khomeini gave on June 3, 1963, which was harshly critical of the shah. "You wretched, miserable man," Khomeini said, "forty-five years of your life have passed. Isn't it time for you to think and reflect a little, to ponder about where all this is leading you? . . . You don't know whether the situation will change one day nor whether those who surround you will remain your friends."[6]

Two days later, the 60-year-old Khomeini was arrested. His arrest sparked a three-day protest in which shopkeepers, religious leaders, office workers, teachers, students, factory workers, and tens of thousands of others marched in the streets of Tehran, Qom, and four other major Iranian cities. Government buildings were stormed; stores were set on fire.

Khomeini's face was on posters plastered everywhere. The shah was finally forced to send in the military, which violently attacked the demonstrators. Estimates are that several hundred people were killed and millions of dollars of property was destroyed before the unrest finally ended.

Khomeini had become a symbol for those opposed to the shah's policies. Without meaningful political parties, free elections, or opposition newspapers, most Iranians turned to support of Khomeini as the only way to protest the reign of the shah.

The shah's decision in 1964 to sign an agreement with the United States granting diplomatic immunity to all American

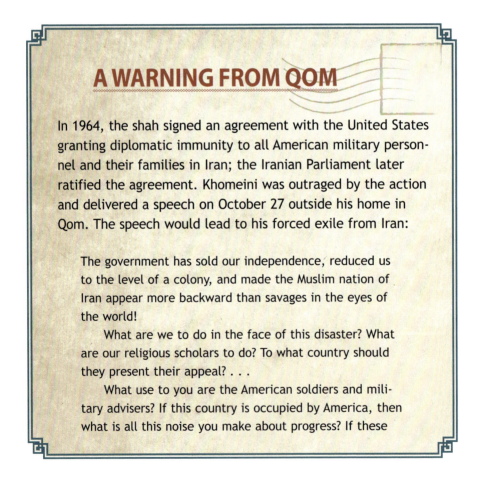

A WARNING FROM QOM

In 1964, the shah signed an agreement with the United States granting diplomatic immunity to all American military personnel and their families in Iran; the Iranian Parliament later ratified the agreement. Khomeini was outraged by the action and delivered a speech on October 27 outside his home in Qom. The speech would lead to his forced exile from Iran:

> The government has sold our independence, reduced us to the level of a colony, and made the Muslim nation of Iran appear more backward than savages in the eyes of the world!
>
> What are we to do in the face of this disaster? What are our religious scholars to do? To what country should they present their appeal? . . .
>
> What use to you are the American soldiers and military advisers? If this country is occupied by America, then what is all this noise you make about progress? If these

military personnel and their dependents in Iran added to the climate of anger with the shah and the United States. Essentially this meant that, should these Americans commit a crime on Iranian soil, they could not be arrested or tried by Iranian courts, but instead they could be tried only by American courts. This sparked intense anger among the Iranian public, reminding them of the special status granted to the British in Iran in the nineteenth century. Khomeini seized on the agreement to launch another attack, publicly complaining, "They have reduced the Iranian people to a level lower than that of an American dog. If someone runs over a dog belonging to an American, he will be prosecuted. But if an American cook runs

advisers are to be your servants, then why do you treat them like something superior to masters? If they are servants, why not treat them as such? If they are your employees, then why not treat them as any other government treats its employees? If our country is now occupied by the U.S., then tell us outright and throw us out of this country! . . .

This is high treason! O God, they have committed treason against this country. O God, this government has committed treason against the Koran. All the members of both houses who gave their agreement to this affair are traitors. Those old men in the Senate are traitors, and all those in the lower house who voted in favor of this affair are traitors. They are not our representatives. The whole world must know that they are not the representatives of Iran. Or, suppose they are; now I dismiss them. They are dismissed from their posts and all the bills they have passed up until now are invalid.*

*Imam Khomeini, *Islam and Revolution: Writings and Declarations*. London: KPI, 1981, pp. 182, 184-185, 187-188.

over the Shah, the head of state, no one will have the right to interfere with him."[7]

The shah had finally had enough of the troublesome ayatollah. He exiled him from Iran, sending him first to Turkey, then in 1965 to Iraq, where he would remain until seeking asylum in France in 1978.

RAPID GROWTH

During the 1960s, the shah oversaw an effort to rapidly industrialize Iran, to build factories to ensure that goods no longer needed to be imported to Iran; instead they could be produced within its borders. Massive construction projects were launched in Tehran. Roads, dams, railways, airports, and hospitals were built.

Oil output also increased, ensuring even greater revenue for Iran. That was a result of the shah's efforts, rather than that of the oil companies. When OPEC, the Organization of the Petroleum Exporting Countries, was founded in 1960, Iran was one of the smallest oil producers of its members. By 1967, it was one of the largest. The shah saw Iran's oil as a way for the country to influence global politics, and he continued to press for greater output and greater revenue from Iran's resource.

But not everyone benefited from Iran's growing riches. The gap between rich and poor increased. Students were similarly alienated. A large number of universities had been built in the 1960s and early 1970s, and it was here that many of the protests against the shah would be launched. As educational opportunities increased and the economy grew, unemployment remained high. Students who had been trained with specific skills found it difficult to find work of any kind. The shah's security forces responded to the campus protests with brutal attacks.

Sattareh Farman Farmaian, who had attended a university in the United States and then returned to Iran to open a school for social workers, noted how unsettling the rapid change was to many Iranians. Worse still was the sense that traditional values were being replaced with Western values of materialism. "A sour anger and discontent, not only with the government but with many aspects of life in our country, had been seething for years," she wrote, "and while fear of SAVAK and the army had stifled it, it had never disappeared. Increasingly, with so many yearning for the new material goods and thinking only of how the country's growing wealth could benefit *them*, Iranians were more inclined to envy and resent those who had achieved success than to emulate people who wanted to do something for their community, and this envy was growing stronger all the time."[8]

PERSEPOLIS

The shah seemed unaware of this growing climate of unrest as he chose increasingly elaborate and expensive celebrations to mark his reign. On October 26, 1967, the day of his forty-eighth birthday, the shah ordered a coronation ceremony (even though he had ruled Iran for some 26 years). He and his wife, Farah, rode in a gilded coach drawn by white horses to the ceremony, where the shah placed a jeweled crown on his head and gave himself the title "King of Kings." He then placed a crown on his wife's head and named her empress and regent for their six-year-old son in the event that the shah should die before his son was old enough to assume the throne.

The shah, in contrast to the modernization campaign he envisioned for his country, looked backward when it came to his own monarchy, attempting to link his rule with that of the rulers of ancient Persia. It was a kind of rewriting of Iran's history, linking the Pahlavi family to the kings of ancient Persia, and a history in which Islam played a very minor role. Finally, the shah decided to stage a spectacular ceremony to celebrate the mythical two thousand and five hundredth anniversary of the Iranian monarchy. The ceremony was to be held in southwest Iran, the capital of the ancient kings of Persia, a

In 1967, despite having ruled Iran for 26 years, the shah of Iran gave himself an elaborate coronation ceremony. Here, he poses with his son, Prince Reza, and his wife, Farah, while wearing the crown, jewels, and embroidered robes used during the coronation.

bare plain where Cyrus the Great once had built his palace. The palace had long since vanished, leaving only excavated remains of ancient columns showing where it once had stood in the sixth century B.C.

The ceremony was scheduled to begin on October 15, 1971, giving the guests—kings, presidents, and international dignitaries—the opportunity to join the shah in celebrating his 30 years of rule in Iran and the tenth anniversary of the White Revolution. The gala was unbelievably lavish and extravagant. The most favored guests were housed in 50 private tents made from beige and royal blue cloth. They were air-conditioned and featured two bedrooms, elegant European furniture, and American plumbing. An Imperial Reception Hall was erected, where the shah and empress hosted dinners and receptions under crystal chandeliers. French chefs were brought in to prepare lavish meals featuring French food and wine. Special linens, crystal goblets, china place settings, and uniforms for the shah's attendants were all commissioned for the occasion. There were fireworks and a spectacular sound and light demonstration. The price tag for the celebration was estimated to be more than $100 million.

In her memoir, Empress Farah defended the elaborate celebration for the awareness of Iranian history and culture it brought to the world. She also noted the criticism sparked by the Persepolis gala:

> The "resistance" of some (clerics and large landowners) and the impatience of others (students and intellectuals), although from opposite ends of the spectrum, would together fuel the growing discontent from 1976 to 1977, leading to our departure and the coming of the Islamic Republic. But in 1971 these reactions did not worry the king: he thought they were usual in a country undergoing profound change and he put his faith in the fruits of progress to free our society, satisfy expectations, and reconcile extremes.[9]

The Persepolis celebration did spark a response from Ayatollah Khomeini, issued from the Shiite city of Najaf in Iraq, where he was living in exile. Khomeini continued to deliver fiery speeches denouncing the shah and his policies, many of which were copied and then smuggled back into Iran, ensuring that he continued to reach a wide audience. Khomeini had begun to specifically call for the overthrow of the Pahlavi dynasty and for the creation of an Islamic government in its place.

In response to the gala at Persepolis, Khomeini labeled the shah an enemy of Islam. "Anyone who organizes or participates in these festivals is a traitor to Islam and the Iranian nation," he said. "Islam is fundamentally opposed to the whole notion of monarchy."[10]

Although the shah dismissed Khomeini's words, many in Iran were listening.

5

Rumors of Revolt

The 1970s were a time of unparalleled prosperity in Iran. In 1971, at an OPEC meeting in Tehran, the shah had argued that the OPEC member nations should change the price structure of oil to bring more money to the producers, rather than to the companies that marketed the oil. This led to a sharp worldwide increase in the price of oil. Oil prices rose even more dramatically two years later, when Arab countries launched an oil embargo against the United States following America's assistance to Israel during the 1973 Arab-Israeli War. Because Iran was not part of this boycott, it continued to ship oil to the United States.

The higher price of oil brought millions of dollars to Iran, which expanded its oil output just as the prices were rising. The shah used much of the windfall to purchase military equipment and weapons from the United States. At the same time, he increased his efforts to modernize and industrialize Iran, causing a dramatic transformation in Iran from a rural to an urban society. In 1956, 56 percent of Iranians worked in agriculture; by 1976 that number had fallen to just one-third.[1] Millions of people moved from rural areas to the cities, creating overcrowding and housing shortages.

Inflation also rose dramatically during this period. The cost of most basic goods nearly doubled between 1973 and 1978, and even for relatively well-off members of Iran's middle class, the cost of living became challenging.[2] More children and young people were being educated, but they found few job opportunities when they completed secondary school or university. For most Iranians, this led to a sense of dissatisfaction and unmet expectations. "Nobody could keep up with inflation," writes Sattareh Farman Farmaian, who was directing a college at the time, "yet those who did not have everything they wanted—and people now wanted *everything*—sulked and gnawed themselves in envy, feeling that they were not getting their due."[3]

In March 1975, the shah decided to establish a single political party for Iran, to be known as the Resurgence Party, or *Rastakhiz*. All Iranian adults were forced to join, or they would be expelled from the country. It was the beginning of a clamping down on freedom of thought and expression. Iranians previously had believed that, even if they disagreed with the shah's policies, as long as they did not actively speak out in protest against them, they would not be in danger. But with the forced enrollment in the Resurgence Party, the shah was demanding that all Iranians publicly declare their support for him and his government.

SAVAK, the shah's secret police, enforced the support for the new party. It was no longer possible to stay out of jail by not openly criticizing the shah. Now, those who were thought to have failed in appropriately praising the shah and his White Revolution—writers, teachers, artists, and intellectuals—were beaten or jailed, tortured, and forced into staged "confessions" of their crimes in public. "Dignity was what SAVAK deprived the nation of the most," writes Roya Hakakian, who was a girl in Tehran at the time. "Beneath its blade, every thinking person split into two: one lived as a private citizen at home; the other lived as a con artist in public, scheming to stay under the agency's radar. To escape its ominous attention, every citizen hid what was on his mind and learned to talk in such a way that his true thoughts would not be obvious."[4]

The shah added to the sense of uncertainty by deciding, in 1976, to change the way that Iranians measured the passage of time by altering the calendar. At the time, Iranians were using the Islamic calendar, which measured years dating back to the time of Muhammad. The shah decided that a new calendar should be used, one in which time was measured from the date when Cyrus the Great established his Persian Empire. Suddenly, the year changed from 1355 to 2535. It was viewed as an attack on the clergy—the shah was announcing that the Muslim calendar had no value in modern Iran.

VOICES OF PROTEST

A group of leading Iranian intellectuals drafted a letter to the shah, asking him to respond to human-rights abuses in his land. The letter also asked him to abolish some of the more oppressive policies he had adopted: the forced membership in a single political party, the restrictions on the press, and the limits on freedom of expression. It was a sign—one that the shah chose to ignore—that opposition to his rule was building across a wide spectrum of Iranians, from the well educated and the wealthy landowners, to the Shiite clerics who objected to the westernization of Iran, to the lower-class citizens to whom the promises of the White Revolution had brought little change.

The world witnessed the growing opposition to the shah in November 1977, when U.S. president Jimmy Carter invited the shah to visit Washington, D.C. Protestors demonstrated outside

From left to right, the shah of Iran, President Jimmy Carter, Empress Farah, and First Lady Rosalynn Carter stand together at the White House in Washington, D.C., on November 5, 1977.

the White House, while students held rallies in Tehran and other Iranian cities. Iranian writer Azar Nafisi, who was living in America at the time and participated in the demonstration outside the White House, describes a gathering of some 2,000 students carrying signs and shouting out slogans: "Death to the Shah; CIA agents, U.S. advisors out of Iran; Iran the next Vietnam; U.S. get out of Iran."[5] President Carter seemed oblivious to the intensity of the anti-shah fervor in Iran. A few weeks after the shah's visit, Carter traveled to Tehran for a New Year's celebration. He toasted the shah, stating that Iran was "an island of stability. . . . A great tribute to . . . the respect and the admiration and the love which your people give to you."[6]

The U.S. presence in Iran had become an increasing source of conflict. Because of instability in the Middle East and Iran's oil resources, American presidents for many years had been eager to court the shah and provide him with the military and political support he needed. American diplomats and CIA agents were highly visible in Iran, particularly in Tehran, and they lived in a manner that was vastly superior to that of the average Iranian, with whom they made little effort to associate. In fact, Americans lived essentially separate lives in Tehran, working in the vast American embassy (which occupied some 27 acres [11 hectares] in the center of the city), shopping in stores stocked with American goods, and enjoying American films and restaurants in their own private enclave. They were not subject to Iranian law enforcement, nor did they pay taxes in Iran.

What was perhaps most offensive to traditional Iranians and the Shiite clerics was the fact that Americans living in Iran openly ignored the customs and traditions of Iranian society. With their behavior and clothing, they demonstrated insensitivity to the country in which they lived and worked, and their attitude helped sow the seeds for an increasing anti-American sentiment that accompanied the rise of anti-shah fervor. Azar Nafisi, a professor of literature at the time of the Iranian Revolution, writes of the anti-Western attitude that was common among some of her students. In *Reading Lolita in Tehran*, she writes of one of her students passionately stating what would become a central theme in the criticism of the West: "All through this revolution we have talked about the fact that the West is our enemy, it is the Great Satan, not because of its military might, not because of its economic power, but because of . . . its sinister assault on the very roots of our culture."[7]

Ayatollah Khomeini was one of the most vocal critics of the shah and his American allies. President Carter's praise of the shah proved a catalyst, giving Khomeini ammunition in his charge that the United States supported human rights only when it had no other military or commercial interests. Soon after Khomeini made this charge, an article appeared in a state-supported newspaper attacking the cleric, suggesting he was a foreigner, a British spy, and a drunk. Many believed the article was published at the request of the shah. It quickly led to riots in the city of Qom, which had become Iran's religious center. During clashes with police, six rioters were killed.

The article's publication was a serious mistake for the shah, if indeed he was behind it. First, most Iranians—even those who disagreed with Khomeini—believed him to be a devout religious figure who should not have been described in such slanderous terms. Next, it linked Khomeini with all of the protests that had been going on in Iran in the 1970s—in fact, it gave him as much stature and visibility as if he had personally headed up all the protests. It turned him into a symbol of the revolution.

By elevating Khomeini in this way, the debate about Iran's future—the debate that would ultimately lead to revolution—became a conflict between Khomeini and the shah. Khomeini had been calling for the shah to be ousted from Iran for several years. Making Khomeini the head of the revolt made it inevitable that, should the revolt succeed, the monarchy would be brought down. And because his speeches had sharply criticized the role the United States was playing in Iran, Khomeini's elevation ensured that as the ayatollah moved to a larger role in the simmering revolution, more of its focus would be anti-American.

STRIKES AND PROTESTS

Protests routinely broke out through much of Iran in the late 1970s. The shah and his military typically responded with brutal force, sparking more protests against the violence. Strikes paralyzed businesses. The shah seemed helpless to restore order. And from Iraq, Ayatollah Khomeini continued to issue statements urging that the shah be overthrown and an Islamic regime set up in place of the monarchy.

Finally, Iranian government officials began to pressure the Iraqi government to silence Khomeini. The Iraqi government was willing to cooperate—there was a large Shiite population in Iraq, and there was concern that Khomeini's talk urging the overthrow of the government might stir up protests in Iraq as well as Iran. In October 1978, the Iraqi government expelled Khomeini. He sought refuge in Kuwait but was refused entry. He next turned to France.

France's president, Valery Giscard d'Estaing, asked the shah if he would object to France allowing Khomeini to enter the country. The shah, believing that Khomeini was a threat principally because he was so close—just across the border in neighboring Iraq—thought that Iran's stability would be better served if Khomeini relocated to distant France. In his memoir, the shah noted, "I lacked the power to line up the world in a solid phalanx against a frail and crazy old man. I could hear the thunder in the Western media should I attempt any action so harsh."[8]

In France, Khomeini soon was in contact with a network of supporters skilled in the use of Western media, and he rapidly established contacts at international newspapers that routinely published his criticisms of the shah. He had access to television and radio reporters who beamed his speeches to supporters around the world. Within Iran's borders, Khomeini could be heard on the BBC, and tape recordings of his sermons continued to be smuggled into the country by supporters.

Perhaps more importantly, Khomeini was able to present a reasonable face to the world from the sunny garden of his home in France. There, he spoke in measured tones, creating an image not of a violent revolutionary but of a scholarly, devout

(continues on page 60)

MESSAGE FROM FRANCE

On November 23, 1978, Khomeini issued a declaration from France—one of many that helped fan revolutionary flames in Iran. In the declaration, Khomeini urged his supporters to rise up against the shah, linking him to ancient tyrants, and making clear to all Iranians that there could be no neutral position in the coming conflict, as shown in this excerpt:

> The history of Iran is witnessing today the most sensitive days that Islam and our dear Muslims have experienced. Today, great nation, you have come to a fork in the road: one way leads to eternal dignity and splendor, and the other (God forbid), to perpetual humiliation and degradation.
>
> There is no excuse for any class of people in the nation to remain inactive today; silence and apathy mean suicide, or even aid to the tyrannical regime. To abandon the straightforward path of the nation and Islam would be treason to Islam and the nation, and support for the enemies of Islam and the nation. The traitors who imagine that they can defeat this Islamic movement and save the Shah by keeping silent, or in some cases even moving to support his tyrannical regime, are mistaken. For now it is too late, and the Shah is on his way out; no one can save the Shah by selling himself. Even if he were to be saved, he would not remain loyal to those who saved him, as we can all see.
>
> I extend a hand of affection and devotion to the noble people of Iran, who, with power they derive from Islam, have given a heavy punch in the mouth to the Shah and his supporters. The martyrs Iran has offered, for the sake of justice and divine aims, I regard as an eternal source of pride. I offer my congratulations to

On December 16, 1978, a mullah and other residents of
Tehran read the latest words from their leader, the Ayatollah
Khomeini, who was exiled in Paris. His message was nailed on
the mosque wall each day for the faithful to read. While 3,000
miles from home, Khomeini influenced millions in the months
leading up to the Iranian Revolution.

the mothers and fathers of those youths who have given
their lives for the cause of Islam and freedom. I envy
those dear, noble youths who have sacrificed themselves
for the sake of the Friend.

The echo of the great Iranian Revolution is rever-
berating throughout the Islamic world as well as other
countries, and it is a source of pride to them, too.
Noble nation, you have alerted the noble young people
of other Islamic nations, and we may hope that your
powerful hand will raise up the proud banner of Islam in
all regions.*

---

*Imam Khomeini, *Islam and Revolution: Writings and
Declarations*. London: KPI, 1981, p. 245.

(continued from page 57)

old man who wanted a more just and democratic society for his homeland.

Sattareh Farman Farmaian writes of seeing a "simmering rage" on the streets of Tehran at this time. More young men were wearing facial hair or beards, as well as buttoned shirts without ties, as a symbolic rejection of Western ways and a demonstration of their Muslim values. But for Farmaian the greatest shock came when she entered the introductory course in social work that she taught to see, among the brightly colored dresses of the female students, a young woman covered from head to foot in black: black sweater, black shirt, and thick black stockings, her hair tucked under a tight black scarf. For Farmaian, there was a strange paradox in a young woman choosing to be educated and studying a modern profession, yet also choosing to be dressed in the garments of an older generation, a generation in which women were not educated. "The very air seemed to have become poisoned by all the frustration and anger," Farmaian notes in her memoir, *Daughter of Persia*, "and I and everyone else felt constantly on edge."[9]

Yet there was excitement also, and a strange and new hopefulness, for Farmaian and all Iranians. Their country was on the verge of a dramatic change. Revolution was in the air.

6

The Revolution Begins

The speeches of Ayatollah Khomeini would become the voice of the revolution, his words whispered by supporters and smuggled tapes of his sermons played quietly in homes around Iran. His supporters called him "*agha*," meaning "master," and would repeat to each other the theme Khomeini stated: The people must get rid of the shah.

Dissatisfaction with the shah had spread throughout many classes in Iran. At mosques, as ordinary people gathered to pray and celebrate religious holidays, their religious leaders spread the message that Iran must return to its Islamic roots, that the shah must be overthrown.

In September 1978, at the end of Ramadan, the Muslim month of fasting and inner reflection, Iran's religious leaders organized a large-scale gathering for prayer. The meeting in

On September 8, 1978, the shah's troops opened fire on protesters in Jaleh Square in Tehran. Now known as Black Friday in Iran, the event proved to be one of the key catalysts in sparking the overthrow of the shah.

Tehran drew some 100,000 people, who marched through the streets chanting their support for Khomeini. The protests lasted three days, and the cries turned from support for Khomeini to calls for the shah's overthrow.

What no one in Iran (apart from the shah's closest family and his doctor) knew was that the shah was gravely ill with cancer. Weak from his battle with the disease, the shah had become increasingly indecisive. Finally, he declared martial law, but the protestors refused to disperse. On September 8, protestors once more gathered near Jaleh Square, in a working-class neighborhood of Tehran. Government troops opened fire; estimates are that 88 people were killed, and the massacre became known as "Black Friday."

Sattareh Farman Farmaian points to the events of Black Friday as a critical turning point for moderate Iranians who had hoped for a peaceful resolution to the crisis. It no longer seemed possible to support a shah whose army would open fire on its own people. "In every town and city," she writes, "neighborhood *komitehs*, or committees, of bearded young men, organized through the mosques, went from house to house, urging people to join the protests, handing out pamphlets and cassettes of Ayatollah Khomeini's sermons. Strikes spread through the country to oilfields and refineries, chemical works, and other important industries. The mass demonstrations continued without interruption."[1]

Maintaining normal daily routines in Iran became impossible. The strikes spread to banks, newspapers, and post offices. The shah tried to appease his people in a series of increasingly ineffective steps—by dismissing some of his government officials and replacing them with others; by releasing certain political prisoners. He turned to his American allies, but their advice was conflicting, reflecting the different views on Iranian policy within President Carter's cabinet.

The violence soon spread. European shops and businesses associated with the West were set on fire. Foreign banks and the British embassy were similarly targeted. Barricades constructed from tires, abandoned cars, and debris from construction sites were set up in the streets of Tehran, designed to make it impossible for the army's tanks to maneuver. Many of those who had supported the shah began to leave the country. Soon, frightened by the rising violence, others joined them: doctors, businessmen, and many who had been educated in Western schools.

CHAOS AND CONFUSION

By December 1978, the violence in Iran seemed out of control. Khomeini's speeches from Paris urged the people of Iran to unite and sacrifice themselves until they had persuaded the shah's army to join their cause. The streets of Tehran filled with crowds, women dressed in black veils and angry men waving fists and carrying banners. The crowds, sometimes made up of thousands of people, would shout slogans. The streets were marked by shuttered, empty, burned-out stores; overturned cars and trucks, flashing police lights; and the smell of smoke and tear gas.[2]

Gunfire could be heard throughout Tehran. Armed guerrilla fighters had appeared in the capital, riding around in army patrol vehicles and covering their faces in masks. Roya Hakakian was a 12-year-old girl when Tehran erupted into chaos. "What did I understand of the revolution?" she writes in *Journey from the Land of No.*

> Nothing I could put into words. But I recognized it when I saw it. It was in the air.... Rocks were strewn on the pavements. Stray tires flared in the middle of every block. Half-burnt pictures of the royal family littered the streets. Turned-over cars on fire, no longer an oddity, did not draw spectators. Canals carried the debris of the city's gallantry: pamphlets, bloody socks, torn sleeves.[3]

Finally, it became clear that the shah was no longer in control of his country. Even President Jimmy Carter sent him a message urging him to leave Iran. The shah requested that he be given asylum in the United States, and the request was granted. But the shah and Carter's representatives had very different ideas about precisely what was being offered. The shah believed that the situation would prove similar to the crisis in the 1950s when he had briefly left Iran for Italy—he would spend a short time in the United States until events in Iran settled down. During that period he would meet with the American president and top U.S. officials to discuss how they could assist him in reestablishing control in his country.

American officials sensed that this would not be a temporary situation, but instead that the shah needed to be replaced.

Rioters set fires on Tehran's main streets during anti-government demonstrations on November 5, 1978. Many banks and cinemas were burned and damaged in the chaos.

They wanted to begin to build a relationship with whomever would assume power after he had left. To this end, they wanted to encourage the shah to leave Iran quickly, and then to guarantee that he maintain a low profile so that a new government could assume control. Their plan was to bring him into the United States, not to Washington but to a remote air base along the East Coast; from there he would travel to California, where a large estate had been arranged for him in Palm Springs. Their mistaken belief was that, by providing a home for the shah, they would be assisting the new Iranian government.

On January 16, 1979, the shah and Empress Farah left Iran. The shah had appointed a new prime minister, Shahpur

Bakhtiar. At the airport he announced that he was leaving the country for a brief rest and placing the government in Bakhtiar's hands. "My memory of this last encounter is one of unbearable emotion," writes Empress Farah.

> The men present were officers, pilots, members of the court, and the Imperial Guard who had all shown great courage, and yet on this occasion one could feel their extreme distress. One after the other, they kissed the king's hand, their faces bathed in tears. Even Mr. Bakhtiar who was in favor of our leaving had tears in his eyes.[4]

Sobbing could be heard as the shah and empress climbed the steps to the plane. Shortly after 2:00 P.M., the plane took off from Tehran and headed west. In his memoir, the shah recalled: "The last image which I carried of this land over which I had reigned for thirty-seven years and to which I had offered a little of my blood was that of the frightful distress on the tearful faces of those who had come to bid us farewell."[5]

The small group at the airport was beginning a tragic journey. The shah would spend the final months of his life attempting to receive asylum from a collection of foreign leaders before finally losing his battle with cancer on July 27, 1980. The military officials who wept as he left the country would soon lose their lives, along with any others seen as too closely connected to the shah. Bakhtiar would serve as prime minister for only a month before he was forced to flee for his life to Paris. He would be assassinated there in 1991.

THE SHAH HAS GONE

As news of the shah's departure was broadcast in Tehran, the capital erupted in celebration. Statues of the shah were torn down. Car horns blared. People waved posters of Khomeini. Newspapers blared the headline: "THE SHAH HAS GONE."

But beneath the celebration was a feeling of uncertainty. Iran had been a monarchy for 3,000 years. Who or what would replace the shah? He had not, after all, announced that he was abdicating—merely that he was leaving the country, traveling to Egypt to visit his friend President Anwar Sadat, and to rest and recover his health. Prime Minister Bakhtiar tried to step into the void by taking measured steps to restore order. He publicly stated that a constitutional form of government would be put into place. He dissolved the dreaded SAVAK. He announced plans for a freer press. He also proclaimed that diplomatic relations with Israel would be cut—a popular move with many Iranians.

Ayatollah Khomeini responded by issuing a statement that cooperation with Bakhtiar was no different than "obedience to Satan."[6] Khomeini's supporters had been publicly calling for an end to his exile, for him to be given permission to return to Iran. Bakhtiar, knowing that Khomeini's return would make it impossible for him to restore order in the country, tried to negotiate with Khomeini to remain in France until order had been restored. Khomeini refused and instructed his supporters to prevent Bakhtiar's government officials from entering their offices. Once more crowds moved through the streets of Iran, this time calling for Bakhtiar to resign. Finally, with popular pressure growing too strong, Bakhtiar was forced to allow Khomeini to return. On February 1, 1979, after 14 years in exile, Khomeini came back to Iran. More than a million Iranians gathered to welcome him home.

TEN DAYS

The excitement that swept through Iran upon Khomeini's return infected even the most skeptical. "Not in almost thirty years, since the nationalization of our oil by Mossadegh, had Iranians felt so joyous, so united in a common emotion, as at this moment," notes Sattareh Farman Farmaian. "An extraordinary euphoria flooded the entire nation. . . . Without being able to say quite how, we felt that Ayatollah Khomeini's return would make us a better people."[7]

Before his return, Khomeini had hinted he would go to Qom when his exile had ended, to resume his teaching and studies. The suggestion was that he would remove himself from politics and serve as a spiritual leader. But it quickly became clear that Khomeini was not going back to Qom. Instead, he set up a temporary headquarters in an old school in the eastern part of Tehran. From there, he instructed his supporters to continue to demonstrate against Bakhtiar's government. He also issued statements warning Iranians to beware the Americans in Iran, who might be CIA spies working to restore the shah to power.

For 10 days, officials from Bakhtiar's government and the remnants of the shah's army struggled with Khomeini's supporters, each attempting to gain control over Iran. On February 5, Khomeini named his own prime minister, Mehdi Bazargan, and ordered him to set up a provisional government. The choice of Bazargan was an astute one. He was viewed as a more moderate Islamist, one with strong ties to the democratic movement. Khomeini's choice helped reassure those more moderate elements in Iran who worried about the kind of government that would replace the shah. Khomeini announced that this provisional government had special authority and must be obeyed. In a press conference on February 5, 1979, Khomeini stated, "I hereby pronounce Bazargan as the Ruler, and since I have appointed him, he must be obeyed. The nation must obey him. This is not an ordinary government. . . . Revolt against God's government is a revolt against God. Revolt against God is blasphemy."[8] Many who had been appointed by Bakhtiar chose to flee the country, fearing for their lives. Civil servants were on strike; offices were empty. Armed guerrilla groups moved through the streets of Tehran, seizing prisons, television and radio stations, and government buildings.

The army was divided. Some members remained loyal to the shah and the government he had appointed when he left. Others supported Khomeini and sympathized with the revolutionary cause. Facing heavily armed civilians, the army found it practically impossible to restore order. By February 11, revolutionary forces controlled most of Tehran's police stations. They broke into armories and distributed weapons to any male who wanted them, then led attacks on the army bases. The military, hampered by confused orders and mass defections, was unable to respond. The Bakhtiar government collapsed, and the prime minister fled for his life.

Khomeini then broadcast a triumphant message to the nation: Iran was now an Islamic state. For the next several weeks, hundreds of officials linked to the shah or Bakhtiar would be executed.

Revolutionary Government

Once the Islamic Republic of Iran had been pronounced, Khomeini began to cement his power by setting up his own military and police forces. These were known as revolutionary committees and revolutionary militia. Their duties were not specific; their power was vast. The revolutionary committees began with a charge to protect communities and help restore order, while arresting opponents to Khomeini. This gradually expanded from arresting supporters of Bakhtiar and the shah to protecting and guarding the public morality—arresting citizens for swearing, for possessing alcoholic beverages, or for playing Western music.

Khomeini called upon Iranians to help restore order. On February 12, 1979, he formally named Bazargan as prime minister of the new government and announced that Muslims must now demonstrate proper discipline. He announced that all banks, offices, and shops would reopen and that schools and universities would resume classes on February 17. Guns obtained during the looting and chaos were to be turned in to the government.

During the next several days, however, burning and looting continued. There were burned-out and boarded-up buildings throughout the capital. Guerrilla groups, many dressed in the military uniforms captured from the army bases, rode through Tehran's streets, fighting with one another for control of neighborhoods. People were being denounced, many falsely, for being supporters of the shah. Anyone with a grievance against a neighbor or co-worker might tell the revolutionary committee that that person was an opponent of the new government, and the person would be thrown into prison.

On February 14, the anti-American mood led to an attack on the American embassy in Tehran. The large, 27-acre (11-hectare) compound in the heart of Tehran included the chancery, the main two-story structure that occupied several city blocks, plus several concrete consular buildings, the ambassador's residence, a residence for the deputy chief of mission, a warehouse, a large commissary, a small office building, and four small staff cottages. Behind the high brick walls the embassy sat in a vast, parklike setting with pine trees and tennis courts, a swimming pool, and a satellite reception center.

Inspired by Khomeini's anti-American speeches, a group of students briefly occupied the American embassy, scaling the walls and disrupting operations until the intervention of Bazargan and his officials persuaded them to leave. Additional defensive measures at the embassy were added: The windows facing the front street were layered with bulletproof plastic panels and sandbags, and the walls were topped by three feet (0.9 meters) of curved and pointed steel bars. But the walls were soon covered with graffiti, spray-painted insults, posters of Khomeini, and revolutionary slogans.

SHADOW GOVERNMENT

While Bazargan was officially Iran's prime minister, there was little doubt that Khomeini was, in reality, Iran's ruler. There were in fact two governments in Iran—the official government, with Bazargan as its head, and the shadow government headed by Khomeini. The result would be a struggle for control of Iran that would last several months and culminate with Khomeini firmly in power.

In the early days of the revolution, Khomeini apparently used Bazargan as a way to ensure broader support for the new form of government being set up to replace the shah. The military, the moderate and liberal citizens, and those who supported a democratic form of government were assured by Bazargan, who spoke publicly of the need to reestablish laws and respect for human rights in the new Iran.

Bazargan, in an effort to create a constitutional framework for the new government, called for a public referendum to allow Iran's citizens to decide what form of government the new Iran would adopt. Khomeini intervened behind the scenes to ensure that the voters were given only one option: They could vote either "yes" or "no" on the question of whether Iran should become an Islamic Republic. Colored ballots were used to ensure that even illiterate Iranians could easily participate. Green ballots were used for the "yes" vote; red ballots were used for a "no" vote. At some polling places, only green ballots were available.

Khomeini then made his wishes clear. He was the first Iranian leader to use television and other media to directly address the Iranian people. On March 1, he appeared on television to warn Iranians, "Though freedom has been achieved, the roots of imperialism and Zionism have not yet been severed. To achieve real independence we have to remove all

A portrait of Ayatollah Khomeini taken in February 1979. Upon his return to Iran, Khomeini began to take control of the apparatus of government in order to create an Islamic republic in Iran.

forms of American influence, whether economic, political, military or cultural. . . . Soon a referendum will be held. I am going to vote for an Islamic republic, and I expect the people to do the same."[1] The details of this Islamic republic and what form its government would take were not made clear before the referendum. Nonetheless, voter turnout was huge, and 97 percent of the electorate voted "yes" for an Islamic republic, a figure the Iranian government would use well into the future as evidence of public support.

Khomeini next turned his efforts to ensuring that Iran was not simply an Islamic republic in name, but in fact. He urged his supporters to ensure that Islamic laws, customs, and morals replaced Western laws and cultural influence. Edicts were sent out that undermined Bazargan's plans, including an instruction to all female employees of the government to "dress in accordance with Islamic code."[2]

Debates over the speed in which change should occur and over the drafting of the constitution for the new republic sharpened the divide between Bazargan and Khomeini. Initial drafts of the constitution called for a government run by experienced civil servants who would receive advice from a council of religious leaders to ensure that the government's policies conformed to the teachings of Islam. Under pressure from Khomeini, that changed. The new Islamic Republic of Iran would contain four branches rather than the three customary in Western governments. In addition to the executive, legislative, and judicial branches, a fourth branch, the Council of Guardians, or the Supreme Council, was added. This council, consisting of 12 religious leaders, would oversee all of the activities of the other three branches. It was the council's job to ensure that all laws passed and all actions taken on behalf of the government complied with Islamic teaching. It had the power to veto any that it believed did not. Any law, action, or activity that the council believed was "anti-Islamic" would be banned.

Rather than the original plans for a strong presidency aided by an advisory council of clerics, the final version of the constitution created a weak presidency with policy firmly shaped by the Supreme Council. At the same time, the Supreme Council was to be headed by a *faqih*, or supreme ruler, who would serve as commander in chief of Iran's armed forces, approve or veto any candidate for political office, and appoint military leaders and judges. He personally would appoint half of the members of the Supreme Council or Council of Guardians. And his term would be unlimited—he could serve as supreme ruler for as long as he wanted.

As the terms of the proposed constitution became public, protest began to spread through Iran. Even some moderate clerics spoke out against the dictatorship that the new constitution would create. Sattareh Farman Farmaian writes of this period:

> Simply walking around Tehran was frightening, for the neighborhoods now belonged to whoever got up earliest and had the most guns. The dozens of new parties and factions that had arisen since February were trying to enforce their supremacy in the streets, and it was common for huge traffic jams to form at large squares and intersections. Here, ten or twenty enraged young men from different parties would be trying to take control of traffic by shouting conflicting instructions at drivers and pedestrians. . . . Summary executions, official and otherwise, were increasing rapidly.[3]

Farmaian herself was arrested. After her release, she went into hiding, then was forced to flee Iran when she learned death threats had been made against her.

THE U.S. EMBASSY IS SEIZED

As the public struggle for control of Iran was playing out, the shah once more assumed a role in the debate. Since leaving Iran, he had traveled from Egypt to Morocco and then on to the Bahamas, but his cancer had spread and he desperately needed medical treatment. The administration of President Jimmy Carter had hoped to build diplomatic relations with the new Iranian government, and so, after initially agreeing to the shah's request for asylum, they had resisted plans to allow the shah to settle in the United States. Finally, on October 22, the shah was allowed to enter New York in order to be admitted to a hospital for treatment. Few people outside of the

Demonstrators burn an American flag atop the wall of the U.S. embassy where Iranian students began holding American hostages on November 4, 1979. Fifty-three Americans would be held hostage for 444 days.

shah's doctors and immediate family knew how far the cancer had spread or how he had deteriorated. When word reached Iran that the shah had been admitted to the United States, many believed that the stated reason—medical treatment—

was simply a ploy in order for the United States to begin a plot to return the shah to power.

Khomeini seized upon this to once more encourage his supporters to rally against the United States. Unfortunately, this increase in anti-American rhetoric coincided with a diplomatic meeting in Algeria. Prime Minister Bazargan traveled there to participate in a celebration marking the anniversary of the Algerian Revolution (1954–1962). U.S. National Security Advisor Zbigniew Brzezinski was also at the meeting, and on November 1 Bazargan and Brzezinski met and were photographed shaking hands. The Iranian media (controlled by Khomeini's supporters) published the photo accompanied by articles darkly hinting of the return of American meddling in Iran's affairs.

On November 4, 1979, the fifteenth anniversary of Khomeini's forced exile and the one-year anniversary of a violent clash between Tehran University students and the shah's forces, a large crowd gathered outside the American embassy. Those working in the embassy did not immediately realize that this protest was different from the many that had preceded it. A large group of Islamic activists, many of them students at Tehran universities, broke through the main gate, then used bolt cutters to break the chains and swing open the doors. Hundreds more immediately flooded into the embassy compound. They had inside information about the most vulnerable access points to the embassy (including the location of an unlocked window), as well as the position of the Marine guards and the area where most of the American diplomats were likely to be found.

The embassy had once had nearly 1,000 staff members, but with the political turmoil in Iran and the February attack on the embassy, many nonessential personnel and their families had been recalled to the United States, and now the embassy staff numbered just slightly more than 60. Not all of them were at the embassy when the attack began; in fact, the most senior

American diplomat in Iran, Bruce Laingen, who was serving as acting ambassador, had left with two staff members for a meeting at the Foreign Ministry.

HOSTAGE CRISIS: DIFFERING VIEWS

For the 52 Americans held captive in Iran for 444 days between November 4, 1979, and January 20, 1981, the seizing of the American embassy marked the beginning of a terrifying nightmare. Many were tortured and beaten. Eight Americans lost their lives in an attempted rescue mission that failed. Several Iranians whose names were mentioned in documents taken from the embassy after it was seized—documents that suggested the Iranians may have assisted the American diplomats or even engaged in spying—were executed.

In the United States, some view the hostage crisis as the first step in a rising tide of anti-Americanism sweeping through the Muslim world. But for many Iranians, the seizure of the embassy is viewed as a success, an inspiring tale of a small, devout group of students who were able, against incredible odds, to storm the gates of an evil superpower and bring it to its knees. For those Iranians committed to an Iran wiped clear of Western influence, the embassy seizure provided the opportunity to firmly eliminate those forces allied with America who suggested that the return of the shah was imminent.

The hostage crisis had important implications for Iran's ability to conduct diplomatic relations with the rest of the world. Mark Bowden describes the taking of the embassy in Tehran as "an assault on diplomacy."* The diplomats and embassy personnel who were held captive were the victims of a crime, and Iran's inability to guarantee their safety

A few staff members were able to slip away when the attack began, but the remaining Americans were seized, blindfolded, bound with cords, and paraded outside. Kathryn Koob, director

On November 9, 1979, one of the U.S. hostages is displayed outside the U.S. embassy in Tehran by the Iranian hostage takers. Although President Carter worked throughout the 1980 presidential campaign to secure their release, the hostages were not freed until Ronald Reagan was inaugurated on January 20, 1981.

would affect its relations with the West for decades. The Iranian government has never renounced the seizure of the embassy and the kidnapping of American diplomats; since that time, the United States has not had diplomatic relations with the Islamic Republic of Iran.

*Mark Bowden, *Guests of the Ayatollah: The First Battle in America's War with Militant Islam.* New York: Atlantic Monthly Press, 2006, p. 595.

of the Iran-American Society in Tehran, was caught and taken to the embassy to join the other hostages. She recalled the terrifying experience as she neared the embassy ground:

> We turned a corner sharply and could hear the mobs in the distance. I knew at once that something was different. The sound was not that of the shrill, happy, exultant cry of the revolutionary victor. Nor was it the polite, shouted slogans of people demonstrating loyalty to a cause. This was the terrifying sound of anger, hatred and mob violence.[4]

KHOMEINI TRIUMPHANT

The seizing of the American embassy and the capturing of 52 Americans as hostages became the final act that would cement Khomeini's control of power in Iran. As soon as word of the attack on the embassy reached him, Bazargan and his administration began working to ensure the hostages' release. But the activists and students who had seized the hostages were supporters of Khomeini and waited for his ruling. If Khomeini condemned the attack on the embassy or ordered the students to immediately release the hostages, they would be forced to comply. Khomeini's condemnation of the attack also would lend his public support to Bazargan's efforts to end the crisis and secure the hostages' release. In effect, he would be publicly supporting and strengthening Bazargan's government.

For two days, the hostages and their captors waited to learn of Khomeini's decision. As they waited, crowds gathered outside the embassy to demonstrate their hatred for the United States. The crowds chanted their support for the captors. Sensitive documents seized from the embassy were read to the crowd from loudspeakers. Trash was carried out in American flags.

On November 6, Tehran Radio broadcast Khomeini's response to the seizure of the hostages. He praised the hostage-takers and gave his blessing to the seizure of the embassy. Soon after Khomeini's public support of the attack, Prime Minister

Bazargan and his government resigned. Within one month, the more conservative version of the constitution passed, granting supreme powers to Khomeini. While some of the hostages initially seized would be released, 52 Americans would be held prisoner for more than a year.

Many Iranians supported those who had seized the American hostages. Sattareh Farman Farmaian notes:

> To the great mass of people, the students' action did not seem the lawless act of terrorism it was, but an assertion of the dignity and independence of Iran. Finally, Iranians felt, after all these years, somebody was expressing their anger, the anger of a people who felt that the great powers had never given them a voice in their own destiny.[5]

8

Islamic Republic of Iran

With Khomeini's firm ascent to power, the political revolution in Iran had come to an end. A cultural revolution soon followed. In April 1980, at the beginning of Ramadan, a strict Islamic dress code was imposed. The laws were changed to include physical punishments specified in the Koran, including lashing, amputation, and death by stoning.

Women were forced to observe the rules of *hijab*, or "covering." They could be beaten if they appeared without the veil, if they showed their hair, or if they wore makeup in public. Only in the privacy of their own homes were women allowed to appear with their heads uncovered. Men's ties—considered too Western—were outlawed. Western music was banned. Journalists could be imprisoned for writing articles deemed critical of Islam.

Azar Nafisi, who was a young woman in Iran at the time of these changes, writes of the violence accompanying the cultural revolution: "Vigilantes attacked unveiled women, sometimes with acid, scissors, and knives.... Religious laws became the law of the land, lowering the legal age of marriage (for women) from eighteen to nine, legalizing polygamy [marriage to more than one wife] . . . , defrocking female judges, and introducing stoning to death as punishment."[1]

According to author Marjane Satrapi, a young girl at the time of the revolution, clothing and grooming reflected one's political position. Fundamentalist women wore the full black chador—the head-to-toe covering. Modern women wore a veil over their hair and a long black coat and dark pants and shoes. "You showed your opposition to the regime by letting a few strands of hair show,"[2] she wrote. Fundamentalist men wore a full beard; progressive men shaved or wore only a mustache.

First names that sounded "too Persian" were discouraged. Street names were changed to reflect Islamic heroes and important dates in the revolution. Universities were shut down in order to make them more "Islamic"—to create a new curriculum and purge them of faculty, students, and staff deemed undesirable. All organizations except Islamic ones were banned from campuses. Women (students and teachers) who refused to wear the veil were expelled. By July, the purging had spread to all areas of Iran. Some 20,000 teachers and 8,000 army officers were dismissed.[3] Khomeini then instituted a series of government regulations that guaranteed his supreme power and the power of the clerics that would follow him after his death. He specified how his succession would be handled when he died—the Supreme Council would meet and choose the next supreme leader.

At the same time, the man who had been brought down by Khomeini lost his final battle—this time with cancer. He had spent his final years of life traveling from place to place, ending his life in Egypt. Egyptian leader Anwar Sadat was the only ally who remained loyal to the end. The shah died on July 27, 1980, and was given a formal ceremonial burial. Apart from President Sadat, only two foreign leaders came to Cairo for the funeral: former U.S. president Richard Nixon and King

SHIRIN EBADI

Shirin Ebadi was born in northwestern Iran in 1947 and moved to Tehran when she was a year old. She earned her law degree from Tehran University and became a judge in 1969, at the age of 22. She was the first female judge to be appointed in Iran.

Disturbed by the human-rights abuses she witnessed under the shah's regime, she initially welcomed the revolution, believing it would help right the many wrongs she saw in her country. A colleague warned her of what the revolution's success would mean for her career, but she did not believe him. Shortly after the revolution's culmination in February 1979, Ebadi and all other female judges were dismissed from their positions. Ebadi was told she could continue to work in the Justice Department, but only as a secretary.

After several months of protest, Ebadi left the Justice Department and tried to practice law, but her request to receive an attorney's license was turned down. She spent several years unable to work until finally, in 1992, she was able to receive the license and could set up her own legal practice.

As a woman operating under the restrictions of the Islamic Republic, Ebadi discovered that few clients wanted

Constantine of Greece. News of the shah's death sparked great celebrations in Iran. With this enemy of the revolution gone, Khomeini encouraged Iranians to place their loyalty not in the state, but in Islam. Increasingly, he was defining Islam as a borderless faith, whose reach extended well beyond the country.

her assistance until she began to build a practice specializing in cases involving human-rights abuses. She has shed light on several murders the Iranian government tried to cover up, representing families of individuals who had been murdered, victims of child abuse, and mothers whose children were taken from them under Iran's child-custody laws. She also has represented several journalists and their families who have been accused or sentenced in relation to freedom of expression.

Ebadi has been imprisoned multiple times for her activities. She is the cofounder of Iran's Association for Support of Children's Rights, and the cofounder and president of the Human Rights Defense Center. She lobbied Iran's Parliament for passage of a law to prohibit all forms of violence against children; the law was ratified in 2002. She was awarded the Nobel Peace Prize in 2003.

Ebadi continues to face danger and intimidation for her work on behalf of Iranian women and children. In December 2008, the Iranian government shut down the Human Rights Defense Center, claiming it was operating without a permit. This action occurred following the office's efforts to assist the United Nations in compiling evidence of human-rights violations in Iran. A few days later, authorities seized Ebadi's computer and confidential records. In January 2009, Ebadi's home was vandalized by a group of young men with ties to the government; police stood by and watched without interfering.

WAR WITH IRAQ

The revolution in Iran had prompted concern among many of Iran's neighbors, who feared that the fiery rhetoric that had led Iran's Shia population to overthrow the shah might inspire similar revolutions among their Shia populations. One of those concerned was Saddam Hussein, the leader of Iraq.

Khomeini added fuel to these fears by publicly stating, "We shall export our revolution to the whole world."[4] Khomeini had maintained many of the contacts he had formed in Iraq during his 14 years in exile there. He was annoyed at the way he had been abruptly expelled from Iraq in 1978 at the request of the shah (Hussein was vice president at the time), and he began calling for Iraq's Shia population to rise up and overthrow the Hussein regime.

Hussein was unsettled by the ayatollah's call on Iraq's Shia population—which forms a majority in Iraq, about 60 percent of the population—to rise up and overthrow him. Tehran Radio began broadcasting messages in Arabic, urging Iraqi Shiites to "accept their responsibility" and "step up their struggle to over-throw the regime of the Shah's heir."[5] Iran set up training camps for Iraqi Shia to school them in guerrilla warfare.

Intermittent clashes began along the 730-mile (1,175-kilometer) border between Iran and Iraq. On September 22, 1980, Iraqi troops launched a full-scale invasion of Iran. The invasion, however, would prove a major miscalculation on the part of Saddam Hussein. He had been misinformed by some of the former Iranian officials who had fled Iran after the revolution: They had told him that ordinary Iranians hated Khomeini and would overthrow him if given the necessary support. Hussein's plan was to seize the oil-rich province of Khuzestan in southwest Iran, along the border with Iraq, and then spark a new revolution in Iran, one that he hoped would result in a government more friendly to Iraq and to Hussein's interests. He also intended to retain control of Khuzestan, whose resources would give him an even greater share of the world's oil.

In October 1980, a Soviet-built tank of Iraq's army prepares to cross the Karoun River as Iraqi troops celebrate their success in the war against Iran. Smoke in the background rises from an Iranian oil pipeline shelled earlier by Iraqi forces. The Iran-Iraq War would not end until 1988.

But Hussein did not imagine Khomeini would use the invasion to rally Iranian support for his government and for the power of Iranian nationalism. Iran had the advantage of numbers—its population was three times that of Iraq—and Khomeini quickly called for a massive conscription of volunteers for the army. Religious leaders in local communities were ordered to begin rounding up volunteers and sending them to the front. Those who might have previously questioned or threatened the government were unified under the common threat posed by the Iraqi invasion. The battle was described in black-and-white terms: Khomeini urged Iranians to drive out the "infidels" threatening Islam.

Iraq initially enjoyed the advantage of a more sophisticated military. Khomeini had deliberately kept the military weak after the revolution to ensure that no elements loyal to the shah could stage a coup and overthrow his regime. The more senior officers, all believed to be loyal to the shah, had been dismissed and, in many cases, executed. In addition to lacking leadership, Iran's military lacked proper equipment. The major military supplier to Iran had been the United States, but with the seizure of the embassy, all military deliveries had been immediately halted. Therefore, much of Iran's military equipment was outdated and in need of repair. What Iran lacked in equipment, though, it made up in manpower, as large groups of Iranians were conscripted and sent to the front to attack Iraqi positions.

The tide of the war gradually turned. By 1982—not even two years after Hussein had sent his troops into Iran—Iraqi forces had been pushed back from Iranian territory. Hussein tried peace negotiations, but the ayatollah refused, and then he called upon Shiites in Iraq to join with the Iranian military to overthrow Hussein's government.

The Iran-Iraq War lasted eight years. Other nations joined the conflict—some of them Arab states, fearing the spread of revolution from Iran to their countries; others, such as some in the West, worrying about substantial amounts of oil

falling under the control of Iran's Islamic Republic. An estimated 300,000 Iranians died in the war; about twice as many
were wounded. For those Iranians not on the battlefield, the
cost of the war was still clear. With resources rationed, there
were periodic shortages of gasoline and electricity. Food was
scarce—prices skyrocketed for such staples as rice, meat, and
butter. Unemployment was high, and the poverty rate grew.

As the war dragged on, many who had hoped for great
things from Iran's revolution found their dreams dashed.
Repression continued, even without SAVAK—in fact, in some
ways it was far worse. Not only did the effort to export the revolution fail, it had cost the country billions of dollars and wasted
hundreds of thousands of lives. Popular support for the war
began to fail. Finally, Khomeini agreed to end the war. On July
20, 1988, he issued a written statement, noting, "I had prom-
ised to fight to the last drop of my blood and to my last breath.
Taking this decision was more deadly than drinking hemlock.
I submitted myself to God's will and drank this drink for His
satisfaction. . . . Today's decision is based only on the interest of
the Islamic Republic."[6]

KHOMEINI DIES

Soon after the war ended, Khomeini's health began to decline.
He was battling cancer, and his eyesight was failing. In his final
months of life he declared a *fatwa* (religious ruling) targeting a
former Muslim from India who was living in England, author
Salman Rushdie. Rushdie had written a novel titled *The Satanic
Verses*, which seemed to question certain Islamic beliefs.

Khomeini broadcast his fatwa on Tehran Radio in February
1989:

> I would like to inform all intrepid Muslims in the world
> that the author of the book *Satanic Verses*, which has been
> compiled, printed, and published in opposition to Islam,
> the Prophet, and the Koran, and those publishers who were
> aware of its contents, are sentenced to death. I call on all

zealous Muslims to execute them quickly, where they find them, so that no one will dare to insult the Islamic sanctities. Whoever is killed on this path will be regarded as a martyr.[7]

Khomeini's edict prompted protests to erupt in Iran against Rushdie and those in the United States and United Kingdom responsible for publishing the book. The British embassy became the target of protests and stones. Rushdie was forced into hiding, and Iran cut off diplomatic relations with Great Britain in response to its refusal to turn the author over to Iranian authorities.

The ruling against Rushdie once more gave Iranians a common enemy against whom to rally. Rather than focusing on the domestic problems of high inflation, unemployment, and food shortages—the aftermath of Iran's war with Iraq—the Iranians were encouraged to unify in support of their ayatollah and against the "forces of evil" in the West. More moderate politicians in Iran, who were tentatively attempting to build alliances with the West, were forced to change their plans.

Khomeini died in Tehran shortly before midnight on June 3, 1989. Iranians were informed by Tehran Radio the following morning at 7:00 A.M. that their leader was gone. A news announcer sobbed as he stated, "The lofty Spirit of Allah has joined the celestial heaven."[8] The government declared 5 national days of mourning, to be followed by 40 days of official mourning. With the exception of essential services, all offices and businesses were closed. People poured into the streets to mourn their leader. Hundreds of thousands traveled to Tehran to attend the funeral, while officials pleaded with the crowds to keep away from Khomeini's home.

It was little more than 10 years earlier that huge crowds had gathered to celebrate Khomeini's return from exile and the successful overthrow of the shah. In that decade, life in Iran had been dramatically transformed: The country had become an Islamic republic that reflected Khomeini's vision, and the ayatollah had become the country's ultimate spiritual and political authority.

Thousands of black-clad mourners surrounded the open coffin containing Khomeini's remains. It was oppressively hot; the Tehran fire brigade sprayed water on the crowd to stop people from fainting. Wailing filled the air. Leading politicians came to pay their last respects to the ayatollah; the crowds made it difficult for them to get close. Khomeini was to be buried in Behesht-e Zahra, the graveyard of the martyrs of the revolution and war, the cemetery he had visited upon first returning to Iran in 1979. But it became impossible for his hearse to move through the streets as the crowds swelled. Several million people assembled, hoping to get a last glimpse of the ayatollah. Finally, the body was taken by helicopter to the graveyard, where a sea of mourners immediately surrounded it.

Grief and emotion overwhelmed many in the crowd, and the mourners pushed toward the litter carrying the coffin. The white shroud covering the body was torn into pieces, and the litter then overturned, spilling Khomeini's body onto the ground. The Revolutionary Guard, Iran's military, was forced to fire shots into the air and beat back the crowd in order to retrieve the body. Finally, the body was loaded back onto the helicopter, which struggled to take off while mourners clung to it. By the time the body was finally buried, Iranian media had reported that more than 10,000 people had suffered injuries, exhaustion, heat stroke, or lost consciousness during this frenzy of mourning; dozens of people lost their lives.[9] Khomeini's exit from the revolutionary stage was just as tumultuous as his arrival had been.

IRAN AFTER KHOMEINI

The day after Khomeini's death, the Supreme Council gathered to read Khomeini's will and to discuss the choice of a successor. The handwritten will, 29 pages long, took three hours to read aloud because of weeping in the audience. The document

On June 3, 2004, Ayatollah Ali Khamenei, the Iranian supreme leader, speaks during a mourning ceremony marking the fifteenth anniversary of the death of Ayatollah Khomeini, at Khomeini's mausoleum, near Tehran, Iran. A picture of Ayatollah Khomeini is hanging at rear.

contained pleas for unity, as well as attacks on the Saudi king and the leadership of the United States. "I hope the nation will march ahead in a determined bid," Khomeini wrote toward the end of his will. "The nation must know that the departure of a servant will not dent the iron bulwark of the nation. There are greater and more honorable servants at your service."[10]

Within 24 hours of Khomeini's death, his successor was named. The choice for supreme leader was the president of Iran, Ali Khamenei. Khamenei was 50 years old and had spent time as a student of Khomeini, although he had not yet earned the title of ayatollah. (He was given it when he was named supreme leader.) He was also an experienced politician. The speaker of the Parliament, Ayatollah Ali Akbar Hashemi Rafsanjani, was sworn in as Iran's new president soon after Khamenei's elevation to supreme leader. Initially, the elevation of Khamenei and Rafsanjani was viewed as a possible moderation of politics in Iran. Rafsanjani was temporarily given the title of commander in chief of the armed forces upon Khomeini's death, but the title soon was returned to Ayatollah Khamenei, a sign that the powers of the presidency continued to be limited.

Khomeini had shaped the revolution, and his teachings and writings continue to shape much of Iranian policy to this day. His successor, Ayatollah Khamenei, has followed Khomeini's teachings, and much of Iran's policy is formulated in an effort to be faithful to Khomeini's vision of Iran and the revolution that brought the Islamic Republic into being.

LEGACY OF A REVOLUTION

The Iranian Revolution began in a spirit of enthusiasm and energy, as a population rose up to overthrow what the people viewed as a corrupt and unresponsive regime. In its place, they envisioned setting up a perfect Muslim community, one that would embrace equality and freedom from oppression.

More than 30 years have passed, but the legacy of the revolution is still clearly felt in Iran. In Tehran, the gleaming, modern city the shah envisioned is gone, replaced by a city of concrete with few tall buildings. Traffic is heavy; the government subsidizes the cost of oil, so gasoline is cheap and plentiful and many people have cars, filling the air with exhaust fumes. Billboards on the walls feature the faces of Khamenei and Khomeini. Murals honor the martyrs of the revolution and the martyrs who died in the Iran-Iraq War.

Power continues to rest in the hands of a single leader— in this case, Ayatollah Khamenei. Like his predecessor, he approves all laws and any candidates for public office. He appoints the 12-member Guardians Council, made up of clerics and judges. The president and elected government of Iran serve at his pleasure; they are the public face of Iran, but Khamenei holds the real power. Writers and artists must be licensed in order for their work to be published or shown. Newspapers and magazines can be shut down if they publish articles deemed "un-Islamic" or critical of the regime.

In the late 1990s, a reform movement briefly sprang up but soon was crushed by Khamenei. When the Iranian Parliament tried to pass legislation that would protect freedom of the press, Khamenei publicly intervened to prevent its passage. Another challenge to Khamenei's hold on power sprang up in June 2009, following the presidential election. President Mahmoud Ahmadinejad, the former mayor of Tehran who had been president since August 2005 and who was seeking reelection, faced a serious challenge from Mir Hossein Mousavi, the opposition leader who had been the Iranian prime minister before that post was abolished in 1989. The announcement that Ahmadinejad had won in a landslide—considered odd because of Mousavi's widespread popularity leading up to the election—sparked suspicion that the government had tampered with the election results in order to engineer a significant victory for the incumbent president. Khamenei's public support of Ahmadinejad, and the Supreme Council's endorsement of the election results, led to massive street protests. The government responded with force. Security forces equipped with guns, tear gas, and batons clashed with the protestors, many of whom were women and young people. An unverified number of people were injured or killed. Mousavi's supporters were arrested, and he was forced into hiding. But the scenes in the streets of Tehran were reminiscent of the 1979 revolution, hinting that the regime's control on power may not be as firm as previously believed.

Iran continues to struggle with many of the same issues that led to the revolution and marked the years that followed it. The role of Islam in Iran and the struggle between modernity and tradition continue to shape public and private debate. The government's response to the needs of its people—for jobs, for food, for security—was an issue at the revolution's dawn and still challenges those who lead Iran. When waning public support for the regime threatens to challenge those leaders, they use violence and repression to bring the people into line. For now, the focus of Iran's leadership is on maintaining a country true to the principles of the 1979 revolution. Their hold on power has not yet been successfully challenged.

The Iranian Revolution brought tremendous change to a people that had known decades of Pahlavi rule. For a brief time, as the country shook off the shah's grip, a vision of a new Iran sprang up among many of its more moderate citizens, but that vision has not been realized. As Roya Hakakian writes:

> It took some time for the clerics to solidify their hold on power, and for Iran to reach that state of despair. But in the interim, the country, especially Tehran, experienced a period of unparalleled freedom. For those who lived in Tehran, that brief period following the revolution remains the most memorable time of their lives. History books speak of the Iranian revolution as one of the greatest revolutions, even the last great revolution, of the twentieth century. The revolution was that and more. For the children of that era, 1979 was not only a year but also a love affair, the most alluring love of their lives. In time, it proved to be the cruelest, too.[11]

CHRONOLOGY

1902	Ayatollah Khomeini is born.
1919	Mohammad Reza Pahlavi is born.
1921	Reza Khan seizes power with British support. Ayatollah Khomeini begins religious studies in Qom.
1926	Reza Pahlavi is crowned shah of Iran.
1941	British and Russian troops occupy Iran during World War II; Reza Pahlavi is deposed and his son, Mohammad Reza Pahlavi, becomes shah.
1951	The Iranian oil industry is nationalized; Mohammed Mosaddeq becomes prime minister.

TIMELINE

1926
Reza Pahlavi is crowned shah of Iran.

1953
The shah flees Iran; aided by the West, the army overthrows Mosaddeq and the shah is restored to power.

1926

1963

1941
British and Russian troops occupy Iran during World War II; Reza Pahlavi is deposed and his son, Mohammad Reza Pahlavi, becomes shah.

1963
The White Revolution is launched.

1951
The Iranian oil industry is nationalized; Mohammed Mosaddeq becomes prime minister.

1953   The shah flees Iran; aided by the West, the army overthrows Mosaddeq and the shah is restored to power.

1963   The White Revolution is launched.

1964   Ayatollah Khomeini is forced into exile following his public criticism of the shah.

1978   Riots and strikes lead to the imposition of martial law. Ayatollah Khomeini seeks asylum in France.

1979   The shah is forced to leave Iran and Ayatollah Khomeini returns. The Islamic Republic of Iran is proclaimed.

1980   The shah dies in Egypt. Iraq invades Iran.

1980
The shah dies in Egypt. Iraq invades Iran.

1979
The shah is forced to leave Iran and Ayatollah Khomeini returns. The Islamic Republic of Iran is proclaimed.

1988
The Iran-Iraq War ends.

1964   1989

1964
Ayatollah Khomeini is forced into exile following his public criticism of the shah.

1989
Ayatollah Khomeini dies. Ali Khamenei becomes supreme leader.

1978
Riots and strikes lead to the imposition of martial law. Ayatollah Khomeini seeks asylum in France.

1988	The Iran-Iraq War ends.
1989	Ayatollah Khomeini dies. Ali Khamenei becomes supreme leader.
2009	Iran celebrates the thirtieth anniversary of the revolution.

NOTES

CHAPTER 1

1. Baqer Moin, *Khomeini: Life of the Ayatollah*. New York: I.B. Tauris & Co. Ltd., 1999, p. 201.
2. BBC, "On This Day: 1 February 1979," http://news.bbc.co.uk/onthisday/hi/dates/stories/february/1/newsid_2521000/2521003.stm.

CHAPTER 2

1. Quoted in David Fromkin, *A Peace to End All Peace: The Fall of the Ottoman Empire and the Creation of the Modern Middle East*. New York: Henry Holt, 1989, p. 460.
2. Mohammad Reza Pahlavi, *Answer to History*. New York: Stein and Day, 1980, p. 54.
3. Ibid., p. 65.
4. Quoted in William Shawcross, *The Shah's Last Ride*. New York: Simon & Schuster, 1988, p. 59.
5. Ibid., p. 70.
6. Mohammad Reza Pahlavi, p. 92.

CHAPTER 3

1. Moin, p. 25.
2. Ibid., p. 28.
3. Ibid., p. 38.
4. Sattareh Farman Farmaian and Dona Munker, *Daughter of Persia: A Woman's Journey from Her Father's Harem Through the Islamic Revolution*. New York: Crown Publishers, 1992, p. 95.

CHAPTER 4

1. Farah Pahlavi, *An Enduring Love: My Life with the Shah*. New York: Hyperion, 2004, p. 73.
2. Kenneth Pollack, *The Persian Puzzle: The Conflict Between Iran and America*. New York: Random House, 2004, p. 75.
3. Patrick Clawson and Michael Rubin, *Eternal Iran: Continuity and Chaos*. New York: Palgrave Macmillan, 2005, p. 70.
4. Quoted in Pollack, p. 88.
5. Quoted in Moin, p. 88.
6. Quoted in Ibid., p. 104.
7. Quoted in Clawson and Rubin, p. 73.
8. Farmaian and Munker, p. 264.
9. Farah Pahlavi, p. 215.
10. Quoted in Shawcross, p. 116.

CHAPTER 5

1. Clawson and Rubin, p. 80.
2. Ibid., p. 81.
3. Farmaian and Munker, p. 278.
4. Roya Hakakian, *Journey from the Land of No: A Girlhood Caught in Revolutionary Iran*. New York: Crown Publishers, 2004, p. 37.
5. Azar Nafisi, *Things I've Been Silent About: Memories*. New York: Random House, 2008, p. 211.
6. Quoted in Shawcross, p. 130.
7. Azar Nafisi, *Reading Lolita in Tehran*. New York: Random House, 2003, p. 126.

8. Mohammad Reza Pahlavi, p. 163.
9. Farmaian and Munker, p. 289.

CHAPTER 6

1. Farmaian and Munker, p. 297.
2. Ibid., p. 311.
3. Hakakian, pp. 121–122.
4. Farah Pahlavi, p. 8.
5. Mohammad Pahlavi, p. 174.
6. Quoted in Clawson and Rubin, p. 93.
7. Farmaian and Munker, p. 324.
8. Quoted in Moin, p. 204.

CHAPTER 7

1. Quoted in Moin, p. 213.
2. Moin, p. 215.
3. Farmaian, pp. 376–377.
4. Kathryn Koob, *Guest of the Revolution: The Triumphant Story of an American Held Hostage in Iran*. Nashville, Tenn.: Thomas Nelson, 1982, p. 36.
5. Farmaian and Munker, p. 391–392.

CHAPTER 8

1. Nafisi, *Things I've Been Silent About*, p. 222.
2. Marjane Satrapi, *Persepolis: The Story of a Childhood*. New York: Pantheon, 2004, p. 75.
3. Clawson and Rubin, p. 96.
4. Quoted in Pollack, p. 183.
5. Quoted in Clawson and Rubin, p. 106.
6. Quoted in Pollack, p. 233.
7. Quoted in Moin, pp. 282–283.
8. Ibid., p. 304.
9. Moin, p. 313.
10. Quoted in Moin, p. 306.
11. Hakakian, p. 8.

BIBLIOGRAPHY

Bowden, Mark. *Guests of the Ayatollah: The First Battle in America's War with Militant Islam.* New York: Atlantic Monthly Press, 2006.

Clawson, Patrick, and Michael Rubin. *Eternal Iran: Continuity and Chaos.* New York: Palgrave Macmillan, 2005.

Energy Information Administration. "Iran: Oil." Available online. URL: http://www.eia.doe.gov/emeu/cabs/Iran/Oil.html.

Farmaian, Sattareh Farman, and Dona Munker. *Daughter of Persia: A Woman's Journey from Her Father's Harem Through the Islamic Revolution.* New York: Crown Publishers, 1992.

Fromkin, David. *A Peace to End All Peace: The Fall of the Ottoman Empire and the Creation of the Modern Middle East.* New York: Henry Holt, 1989.

Gabriel, Satya J. "Class Analysis of the Iranian Revolution of 1979." Available online. URL: http://www.mtholyoke.edu/courses/sgabriel/iran.htm.

Hakakian, Roya. *Journey from the Land of No: A Girlhood Caught in Revolutionary Iran.* New York: Crown Publishers, 2004.

Iran Chamber Society. Available online. URL: http://www.iranchamber.com.

"Iran: Facts and Figures." BBC News. Available online. URL: http://news.bbc.co.uk/2/hi/middle_east/8060167.stm.

Khomeini, Imam. *Islam and Revolution: Writings and Declarations.* London: KPI, 1981.

Koob, Kathryn. *Guest of the Revolution: The Triumphant Story of an American Held Hostage in Iran.* Nashville, Tenn.: Thomas Nelson, 1982.

Linzer, Dafna. "U.S. Urges Financial Sanctions on Iran," *Washington Post*, May 29, 2006, p. A1.

Moin, Baqer. *Khomeini: Life of the Ayatollah*. New York: I.B. Tauris Co. Ltd., 1999.

Mottahedeh, Roy. *The Mantle of the Prophet: Religion and Politics in Iran*. New York: Pantheon Books, 1985.

Nafisi, Azar. *Reading Lolita in Tehran*. New York: Random House, 2003.

———. *Things I've Been Silent About: Memories*. New York: Random House, 2008.

Pahlavi, Farah. *An Enduring Love: My Life with the Shah*. New York: Hyperion, 2004.

Pahlavi, Mohammad Reza. *Answer to History*. New York: Stein and Day, 1980.

Pollack, Kenneth. *The Persian Puzzle: The Conflict Between Iran and America*. New York: Random House, 2004.

Satrapi, Marjane. *Persepolis: The Story of a Childhood*. New York: Pantheon, 2004.

Shawcross, William. *The Shah's Last Ride*. New York: Simon & Schuster, 1988.

FURTHER RESOURCES

BOOKS

Axworthy, Michael. *A History of Iran: Empire of the Mind.* New York: Basic Books, 2008.

Ebadi, Shirin. *Iran Awakening: One Woman's Journey to Reclaim Her Life and Country.* New York: Random House, 2006.

Majd, Hooman. *The Ayatollah Begs to Differ: The Paradox of Modern Iran.* New York: Random House, 2008.

Moaveni, Azadeh. *Lipstick Jihad: A Memoir of Growing Up Iranian in America and American in Iran.* New York: Public Affairs, 2005.

WEB SITES

BBC Iran Country Profile
http://news.bbc.co.uk/1/hi/world/middle_east/country_profiles/790877.stm

Islamic Republic of Iran Broadcasting Service
http://www2.irib.ir

PBS Frontline: Showdown with Iran
http://www.pbs.org/wgbh/pages/frontline/showdown/

PICTURE CREDITS

INDEX

ABOUT THE AUTHOR

HEATHER LEHR WAGNER is a writer and editor. She is the author of more than 40 books exploring political and social issues. She has written several books on the Middle East, including *Iran* in the CREATION OF THE MODERN MIDDLE EAST series published by Chelsea House. She earned a B.A. in political science from Duke University and an M.A. in government from the College of William and Mary.